Human Rights

by William Dudley

Current Issues

San Diego, CA

For more information, contact:
ReferencePoint Press, Inc.
PO Box 27779
San Diego, CA 92198
www. ReferencePointPress.com

Picture credits:
AP Images: 10, 14
Steve Zmina: 32–34, 47–49, 62–65, 78–80

LIBRARY OF CONGRESS CATALOGING-IN-PUBLICATION DATA

Dudley, William, 1964–
    Human rights / by William Dudley.
        p. cm.—(Compact research)
    Includes bibliographical references and index.
    ISBN-13: 978-1-60152-069-2 (hardback)
    ISBN-10: 1-60152-069-7 (hardback)
    1. Human rights. I. Title.
    JC571.D864 2008
    323—dc22
                                                                    2008043424

Contents

Foreword

As modern civilization continues to evolve, its ability to create, store, distribute, and access information expands exponentially. The explosion of information from all media continues to increase at a phenomenal rate. By 2020 some experts predict the worldwide information base will double every 73 days. While access to diverse sources of information and perspectives is paramount to any democratic society, information alone cannot help people gain knowledge and understanding. Information must be organized and presented clearly and succinctly in order to be understood. The challenge in the digital age becomes not the creation of information, but how best to sort, organize, enhance, and present information.

ReferencePoint Press developed the *Compact Research* series with this challenge of the information age in mind. More than any other subject area today, researching current issues can yield vast, diverse, and unqualified information that can be intimidating and overwhelming for even the most advanced and motivated researcher. The *Compact Research* series offers a compact, relevant, intelligent, and conveniently organized collection of information covering a variety of current topics ranging from illegal immigration and methamphetamine to diseases such as anorexia and meningitis.

The series focuses on three types of information: objective single-author narratives, opinion-based primary source quotations, and facts and statistics. The clearly written objective narratives provide context and reliable background information. Primary source quotes are carefully selected and cited, exposing the reader to differing points of view. And facts and statistics sections aid the reader in evaluating perspectives. Presenting these key types of information creates a richer, more balanced learning experience.

For better understanding and convenience, the series enhances information by organizing it into narrower topics and adding design features that make it easy for a reader to identify desired content. For example, in *Compact Research: Illegal Immigration*, a chapter covering the economic impact of illegal immigration has an objective narrative explaining the various ways the economy is impacted, a balanced section of numerous primary source quotes on the topic, followed by facts and full-color illustrations to encourage evaluation of contrasting perspectives.

The ancient Roman philosopher Lucius Annaeus Seneca wrote, "It is quality rather than quantity that matters." More than just a collection of content, the *Compact Research* series is simply committed to creating, finding, organizing, and presenting the most relevant and appropriate amount of information on a current topic in a user-friendly style that invites, intrigues, and fosters understanding.

Human Rights at a Glance

Human Rights Are Universal

While most people agree that human rights apply to all people, regardless of nationality, age, sex, religion, ethnicity, or citizenship status, many countries violate this principle.

Enforcing and Protecting Human Rights

International organizations such as the United Nations have little direct power to enforce treaties or protect rights, which means that this burden falls mainly to national governments.

America's Foreign Policy Priorities

The United States promotes human rights as part of its foreign policy, but some critics question the depth and sincerity of America's commitment to those rights.

Global Awareness of Human Rights

Virtually all of the 192 countries in the world have acknowledged human rights by placing them in national constitutions or signing an international human rights convention. No nation wants to be singled out as a human rights violator.

Failed States

The world's nations have had difficulty dealing with massive human rights violations, including ethnic cleansing and war crimes that take place in failed states—states that have lost control and/or functionality, often due to civil war or unrest.

The War on Terror

The post–September 11, 2001, war on terror waged by the United States (and other nations) has raised significant concerns about whether American safety requires bending or disregarding rules on human rights.

Human Rights and the Global Economy

The existence of more than 2 billion people living in life-threatening poverty without access to food, clean water, and shelter, and the significant gaps in wealth and economic development between the richest and poorest nations, are increasingly being seen as problems that should be addressed within a human rights framework.

Overview

The term "human rights" refers to international norms that define basic legal and moral rights that all human beings possess. Examples of human rights include life, liberty, security of person, equality under the law, the right to a fair trial, freedom of religious and political thought, access to education, basic food and shelter, and freedom from torture and inhumane treatment. The underlying idea behind these and other rights is that all people, regardless of nationality, religion, sex, race, or other characteristics, possess worth and dignity that make them fundamentally deserving of a certain minimum of entitlements and freedoms.

What Are Human Rights?

Human rights differ from the rights a person may have as a member of an organization; such rights are defined and protected by that organization. Persons who are citizens of a nation have certain civil rights by virtue of their citizen status—rights that are defined and protected by that nation's government. Persons possess human rights, on the other hand, simply by virtue of their status as human beings. As such, human rights cannot be surrendered or taken away. People still possess human rights even when they are violated or when local laws or customs disregard them. In other words, they are inalienable.

In America's 1776 Declaration of Independence Thomas Jefferson wrote, "We hold these truths to be self-evident, that all men . . . are endowed by their Creator with certain inalienable rights, that among these are Life, Liberty and the pursuit of Happiness." But the positing of certain fundamental human rights raises the question of who is responsible for upholding and enforcing them. The answer, according to Jefferson, is government, which is "instituted among Men" to "secure these rights." (It was England's failure to do so that justified revolution, according to Jefferson). Since 1776 the idea that humans have natural and fundamental rights has spread throughout the globe, and most nations, including the United States, enshrine at least some human rights protections in their constitutions and legal codes. Of course, this has not always prevented governments from ignoring their laws and disregarding human rights.

> " The underlying idea behind . . . [human] rights is that all people, regardless of nationality, religion, sex, race, or other characteristics, possess worth and dignity that make them fundamentally deserving of a certain minimum of entitlements and freedoms. "

The Beginnings of the Modern Human Rights Movement

One of the most destructive and horrific violations of human rights in history was the Holocaust—the campaign by the Nazi government in Germany in the 1930s and 1940s to systematically isolate, imprison, and ultimately kill millions of Jews and members of other disfavored groups. As the extent of the Holocaust became known as World War II ended, it came to be seen as a grave moral *and* legal crime by those who directly

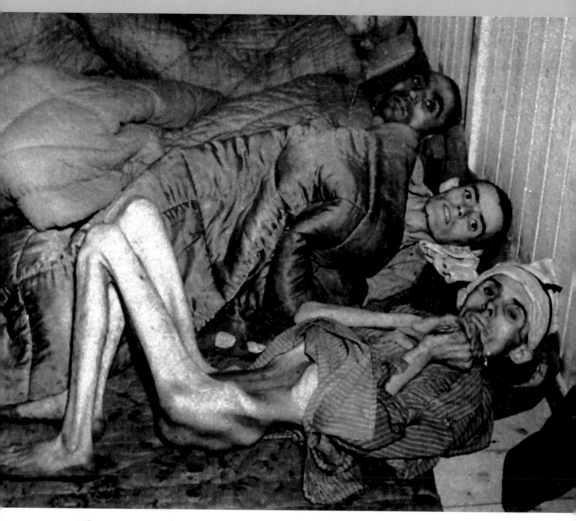

These men were being held in the Buchenwald concentration camp in Germany during the Holocaust. They were clearly grossly mistreated and abused, as were most of the prisoners in the camps. They were rescued in 1945 when American troops liberated the camp.

committed it (regardless of German laws that may have authorized it). But the Holocaust was also seen as a harsh judgment on the rest of the world for not doing more to protect the millions of people who were dehumanized and killed. The conclusion many observers drew was that if national governments could or would not uphold fundamental human rights within their borders, the world community must then step in.

Thus the United Nations (UN) was created in 1945. It is no coincidence that the modern international movement to protect universal human rights and the United Nations were born almost simultaneous-ly—and that both were in part a reaction to the horrors of the Holocaust. The shapers of the post–World War II international order "made the promotion and protection of human rights and fundamental freedoms one of the purposes as well as one of the founding principles of the United Nations," writes political scientist Winston E. Langley. In the decades following World War II, "the idea that protection of human rights knows no international boundaries and that the international community has an obligation to ensure that governments guarantee and protect human rights has gained widespread acceptance."[1]

One of the first actions of the United Nations was to appoint a special committee to draft what became the Universal Declaration of Human Rights. Adopted with no dissenting votes on December 10, 1948, by the General Assembly of the UN, the declaration contained 30 articles defining specific human rights. Its importance, writes Langley, was in establishing "a common standard of achievement for all people and all nations."[2] Since then the United Nations has played a central role in the ongoing debates over human rights and how they should be upheld. Numerous treaties have been negotiated and ratified, both within the auspices of the UN and within various regional bodies, through which most of the world's nations have agreed to protect human rights. However, despite the general consensus on the existence and importance of human rights and governments' responsibility for upholding them, human rights abuses have remained a serious and ongoing problem for many people in many parts of the world.

Where Do Human Rights Come From?

Thomas Jefferson and his American revolutionary peers who helped him write the Declaration of Independence rather cleverly sidestepped the question of where rights such as "the pursuit of happiness" come from by simply asserting that they were "self-evident." But the origins of human rights, the authority on which they are based, and whether they have an existence separate from the laws and treaties that define them, have all been longstanding topics of philosophical debate. Three general theories have been proposed to answer the question of where human rights come from: first, human rights were created by God; second, human rights are inherent in natural law, and third, human rights are social constructs that are created by written laws.

The idea that humans possess rights and inherent dignity because they were so created by God is both enduring and popular, especially in the United States. The Declaration of Independence, written by Thomas Jefferson, refers to humans being "endowed by their Creator" with rights. Jefferson's contemporary, Alexander Hamilton, wrote around the same time that "the sacred rights of mankind" are created "by the hand of divinity itself and can never be erased or obscured by mortal power."[3] These views from America's founding era continue to find expression in more recent times. Civil rights leader Martin Luther King Jr., writing from jail in 1963, asserted that he and other blacks had waited too long for "our constitutional and God-given rights."[4] President George W. Bush in 2002 promised that he would appoint "common-sense judges who understand our rights were derived from God."[5]

> Despite the general consensus on the existence and importance of human rights and governments' responsibility for upholding them, human rights abuses have remained a serious and ongoing problem for many people in many parts of the world.

However, the idea that human rights come from God raises the question of who speaks for God. "God's ambiguous words can be cited for any ideology," argues lawyer and author Alan Dershowitz. "The divine rights of one time and place have repeatedly been recognized as the human wrongs of different times and places."[6] For example, the Bible, the chief source of written religious authority for Christianity, has in the past been used to justify many actions now widely believed to be wrongful violations of human rights, including slavery, wars of conquest, racial discrimination, and the burning of witches and heretics.

Another problem with ascribing the source of human rights to God is that many of the world's people have differing conceptions of God—or do not believe in a deity at all. William Schulz, executive director of the human rights advocacy group Amnesty International USA, wistfully opines that his job would be easier if only "we could prove to the satisfaction of the world that some universally recognized deity had imbued human beings with a set of rights that happened to coincide with . . . the Universal Declaration of Human Rights." But in a world with a diversity of faiths, a religion-based consensus on human rights is impossible to achieve. "If individual people of faith wish to believe that God is the source of human rights, they are welcome to do so," Shulz writes, "but, absent demonstrable proof, their faith is unlikely to be sufficient to convince everyone else."[7]

Natural Law Versus Legal Positivism

An alternative to religious theories of human rights is the concept of natural law. This idea, traced by some back to the philosophers of ancient Greece and Rome, but also expressed by Buddhist, Chinese, Hindu, and other traditions, is that the universe is governed by principles, or laws, and that such laws are not invented but discovered through human reason. Just as the movement of a falling apple and other observations of the physical universe can be explained through scientific theories like Isaac Newton's law of gravity, natural law theorists argue that a moral universe with unchanging laws and realities that govern human life exists. These natural laws provide an external source for the rights written down in constitutions, treaties, and laws.

Political thinkers, including British philosopher John Locke and French philosopher Jean Jacques Rousseau, took the idea of natural law and posited that all humans possess inherent "natural rights" (Locke summed them up as life, liberty, and property.) These ideas in turn inspired the 1776 American Revolution (the Declaration of Independence refers to the "laws of Nature and Nature's God") and the 1789 French Revolution. The influence of the idea of natural law can also be found in the preamble to the 1948 Universal Declaration of Human Rights, which calls for nations to recognize—to accept as self-evident—the "inherent dignity and the equal and

> The idea that humans possess rights and inherent dignity because they were so created by God is both enduring and popular, especially in the United States.

13

These child laborers carry stones to a stone crusher outside of Gauhati, India. While globalization is praised by many as the best way to promote productivity and create wealth, it has also been blamed for accentuating problems of poverty in the world's poorest nations and for creating the conditions for child labor.

inalienable rights of all members of the human family."[8]

But natural law theory has also had critics and detractors. Most note that natural law is—like belief in God—something that cannot be proven to exist and must be simply accepted on faith. Nineteenth-century philosopher Jeremy Bentham colorfully denied the very conception of rights derived from some unchanging essence of humanity as constituting "rhetorical nonsense, nonsense upon stilts." He argued that a true human right "is the child of law; from real law comes real rights; but from imaginary laws, from 'law of nature,' comes imaginary rights."[9] Such a view came to be known as "legal positivism." Those who ascribe to this position believe that human rights simply come from the laws, constitutions, and international treaties written by humans. There is no source external to the law itself, in this view.

What the ultimate source of human rights is thus has no agreed-upon answer. Fortunately, however, the fact remains that people can disagree about the ultimate origins of human rights and yet still agree on such rights' importance and on what those rights are. A growing body of international law created over the past six decades has itself created its own legal reality and forged a general consensus on human rights.

How Can Global Human Rights Be Protected?

National governments hold the primary responsibility for upholding the human rights of their citizens. However, since 1948 the United Nations and other international organizations have tried to assist countries in establishing human rights standards and in upholding human rights.

The 1948 Universal Declaration of Human Rights helped lay the groundwork for dozens of subsequent human rights treaties created by the United Nations. Some of the most important of these treaties include the International Covenant on Civil and Political Rights; the International Covenant on Economic, Social, and Cultural Rights; and the Convention against Torture and Other Cruel, Inhuman, or Degrading Treatment or Punishment. Countries that sign and ratify these treaties are supposed to be legally bound to respect the rights listed in them.

The United Nations, through its various organs, has assisted governments in establishing and maintaining their own legal systems for human rights, investigated and documented violations, and attempted to hold abusers to account. The high commissioner for human rights, a position created in 1993, serves as a full-time coordinator and advocate for human rights work within the UN. The Human Rights Council

> **National governments hold the primary responsibility for upholding the human rights of their citizens.**

(which replaced the Human Rights Commission in 2006) is a 47-member committee of nations charged with promoting human rights, responding to human rights emergencies, and providing direct assistance to UN member states to help them meet their treaty responsibilities. Finally, major policy decisions—such as whether to impose trade sanctions or authorize military intervention against serious and serial human rights violators—are made by the Security Council, a 15-member committee of countries whose five permanent members (the United States, Great Britain, France, Russia, and China) have veto power over all proposed actions.

> The struggle of America and other nations to protect their people from terrorism—while living up to their human rights commitments—is one of several challenges for governments and human rights activists.

Not all work on promoting and protecting human rights is done through the auspices of national governments or the United Nations. Countries in Europe, the Americas, and Africa, working together in regional organizations (one such group is the Organization of American States), have drafted regional human rights treaties and created international courts and commissions to enforce them. Nongovernmental organizations such as Amnesty International and Human Rights Watch work around the globe to investigate and publicize human rights abuses, educate local populations about human rights, work with and provide reports to the United Nations, and lobby for legal reforms in countries with human rights problems.

Should U.S. Foreign Policy Consider Human Rights?

The United States has long prided itself as the "land of liberty," a principled defender and advocate of human rights around the world, and a place where human rights are protected under state and federal laws, including the Constitution and the Bill of Rights. The United States also played an instrumental role in the creation of the United Nations after World War II and the creation and adoption of the Universal Declaration of Human Rights in 1948. Almost 30 years later, President Jimmy Carter declared that human rights would be one of the guiding principles in how America conducts foreign relations with other nations—a commitment that succeeding presidents have not formally refuted. America's State Department includes a specialized bureau on human rights, which researches and files official human rights status reports on all the world's nations on an annual basis.

However, America's commitment to human rights has come under question. Critics argue that the United States' actions often run counter to its words. Other concerns, including trade, national security and counterterrorism, access to natural resources such as petroleum, and simple economic and political stability, often supersede human rights records in determining how America deals with other nations. Whether prioritizing human rights after other concerns is in America's long-term interest is a subject of intense debate.

Human Rights and the War on Terror

Human rights concerns figure prominently in one particular area of U.S. policy—the ongoing controversies surrounding America's reaction to the terrorist attacks of September 11, 2001. Since then the United States has engaged in a "war on terror" that has included military attacks, occupations, and ongoing counterinsurgency operations in Afghanistan and Iraq. This war has also included criminal prosecutions against suspected terrorists, the detention of numerous "enemy combatants" captured in Iraq and other places, serious accusations of their mistreatment and even torture, and the secret electronic eavesdropping on private communications. Many of these policies have been sharply criticized by human rights groups as significant violations of human rights. Some conclude that the United States has tarnished its image by violating human rights treaties it has signed and ratified. But defenders of the United States have maintained that human rights simply must sometimes give way to the protection of American citizens from more terrorist attacks like those that took place in 2001.

What Is the Future of Human Rights?

The struggle of America and other nations to protect their people from terrorism—while living up to their human rights commitments—is one of several challenges for governments and human rights activists. Experts cite several developments and trends that loom large in the future of human rights.

> **National and international laws guaranteeing human rights can be important legal tools in achieving specific social reforms.**

One is the growing recognition of human rights violations in war zones, especially civil wars where formal governments hold little actual control or authority. In the early twenty-first century, war zones in Sudan, Congo, and Iraq have been the scene of serious human rights abuses ranging from genocide and ethnic cleansing to the mistreatment of war prisoners and the creation and displacement of refugees. These crises have intensified discussions over how and whether the world's nations, acting through the United Nations Security Council, can and should intervene in places that are human rights disasters.

Globalization and Education

Another development is globalization—the growing connectivity between the world's financial markets and businesses. While globalization is praised by many as the best way to promote productivity and create wealth, it has also been blamed for accentuating problems of poverty in the world's poorest nations and for creating the conditions for child labor, indentured servitude, and other human rights violations. Some argue that in addition to governments, private transnational corporations and other private organizations must also be held accountable if they are responsible for human rights abusers.

A third development has been the promotion of human rights education and the linkage of human rights with other issues. A goal of education is to teach local citizens to speak out and demand their human rights. Human rights activity has gone far beyond classic human rights issues such as religious liberty, freeing political prisoners, censorship, and fairness in the criminal justice system (although such work continues). Many individuals and organizations devoted to a wide variety of social and political issues—including sexual equality, the environment, children's welfare, economic development, AIDS prevention and treatment, poverty, hunger, and even global warming—have been drawn within the orbit of the global human rights movement, often after receiving human rights education. They have found that the ideas expressed in the Universal Declaration of Human Rights can be a powerful way to frame their appeal for change, and that national and international laws guaranteeing human rights can be important legal tools in achieving specific social reforms.

Sixty years after the adoption of the Universal Declaration of Human Rights, the idea that human rights are important and should be protected has gained global assent and seems to have a secure future. However, as the ongoing debates surrounding America's war on terror and other issues indicate, much controversy still exists over how to translate the ideals into reality.

What Are Human Rights?

66The Universal Declaration of Human Rights, signed 60 years ago, is seen as a great achievement. But there is huge disagreement about which rights matter most.99

—*Economist*, "A Screaming Start; The UN and Human Rights."

66In a world where malnutrition and preventable disease kill more people than wars and state-sponsored repression, it is clear that the concept of human rights is long overdue for a redefinition.99

—Jason Mark, "At the Millennium, a Broader Vision of Human Rights."

If asked, most people (and most governments) would agree with the basic notion that all people have certain inherent rights. However, asking five people exactly what these human rights consist of will probably result in five different answers. Achieving a consensus on what constitutes human rights has been a challenge for the political leaders and others responsible for protecting human rights.

One approach to answering the question, what are human rights? is to simply define them as what people need for a dignified and fulfilling life. "Human rights are rights so basic that people cannot live like human beings without them,"[10] writes journalist and author Gerald S. Snyder. The United Nations once defined human rights as "those conditions of life which allow us fully to develop and use our human qualities of intelligence and conscience and to satisfy our spiritual needs. Human rights

20

are fundamental to our nature; without them, we cannot live as human beings."[11] The usefulness of this approach is limited, however, as people may differ as to what is fundamental to human nature and dignity. As political scientists Julie Harrelson-Stephens and Rhonda L. Callaway point out, these definitions, while useful, fail "to provide any specificity of what actually constitutes a human right."[12]

Interpreting the Universal Declaration of Human Rights

Some specificity can be found in the landmark Universal Declaration of Human Rights (UDHR). The document was produced by a special United Nations committee, led by former American First Lady Eleanor Roosevelt. Members sought input from historians, religious leaders, and ordinary citizens. The resulting document, adopted by the UN General Assembly in 1948, would at first seem to be the authoritative reference on what constitutes human rights. But the nonbinding declaration also left governments free to interpret what those words mean and how to enforce them. Harrelson-Stephens and Callaway note that this has led to "definitions of convenience as states carve out conceptions that serve their best interests." Even as states turned to the UDHR and to subsequent international human rights treaties, they "have opted for the types of enumerated rights that reflect their respective ideologies."[13] In other words, different countries often stress different ideas—or even different definitions—as to what constitutes human rights.

> " The United Nations once defined human rights as 'those conditions of life which allow us fully to develop and use our human qualities of intelligence and conscience and to satisfy our spiritual needs.' "

In analyzing these differing ideas, scholars have placed human rights into three distinct categories; some have referred to these as "three generations" of rights. The first generation of human rights is associated with Western powers such as the United States and Great Britain. The second generation is associated with socialist and Communist nations, especially the Soviet Union and China. The third generation is sometimes associated with developing nations in Africa and Asia that threw off colonial rule in the twentieth century.

First-Generation Rights

Civil and political rights represent the first generation of human rights. They can be traced back in part to eighteenth-century European political theory, especially the ideas of John Locke and other philosophers. Locke, an English political thinker, argued that people had "natural rights" of life, liberty, and property and that people had the right to revolt against governments that violated those rights. Locke's ideas in turn inspired leaders of the 1776 American Revolution and the 1789 French Revolution. Civil and political rights are represented by the first 21 articles of the 1948 Universal Declaration of Human Rights, and include:

- The right to life
- The right not to be subjected to torture or cruel and inhumane treatment
- Freedom from being held in slavery
- Freedom from arbitrary arrest and detention
- The right to be brought before a judge or court if detained
- Freedom of movement and emigration
- The right to equal protection under the law
- Freedom of religion
- Freedom of opinion and expression
- The right of free association
- The right to own property
- The right to take part in one's government and to vote in fair elections

In general, civil and political rights involve rights of the individual to think and act without government opposition or interference. It is recognized that government sometimes should have necessary powers to deprive people of life and liberty for the public interest (for example, imprisoning or executing murderers or traitors), but also that safeguards must be in place to ensure that people are not imprisoned or killed for arbitrary or political reasons. First-generation rights are sometimes called "negative" human rights because they impose prohibitions or limitations on what governments can do.

Abuses of First-Generation Rights

Sadly, contemporary examples of countries abusing political and civil rights are not hard to find. One example is Vietnam, where the Vietnamese Communist Party (VCP) has maintained one-party rule since 1975. The group Human Rights Watch (HRW) in its 2008 annual report on global human rights notes that the government restricts freedoms of speech, press, and expression by controlling all media and by mandating criminal penalties to all "publications, websites, and internet users that disseminate information that opposes the government, threatens national security, or reveals state secrets."[14] Individuals who have used the Internet to participate in pro-democracy discussion forums or to criticize the government have been sent to prison. Leaders of religious groups who refuse to register with the Vietnamese government have also been imprisoned—a harsh measure that represses the right of the Vietnamese people to practice their religious beliefs.

Indeed, the VCP has imprisoned hundreds of Vietnamese citizens in ways inconsistent with human rights standards, according to Human Rights Watch and other observers. Some citizens have been subject to house arrest or placed in mental hospitals. In some cases, detentions have been carried out without any form of trial, contrary to Article 9 of the UDHR. "Lawyer Bui Thi Kim Thanh, who assisted farmers with land rights complaints, was arrested in November 2006 and involuntarily committed to a mental hospital," Human Rights Watch noted in its 2008 report. "She was released in July 2007." Prisoners have also been subjected to harsh treatment and torture in violation of Article 5 of the UDHR, according to HRW. "Prisoners are placed in solitary confinement in dark, unsanitary cells, and there is compelling evidence of torture and ill-treatment of political prisoners, including beatings and electric shock."[15]

> " Sadly, contemporary examples of countries abusing political and civil rights are not hard to find. "

Other nations that have been singled out in recent years as having especially poor records in upholding political and civil rights include Myanmar (Burma), Iran, North Korea, Uzbekistan, and Zimbabwe. In these and other countries, governments maintain a tight control over political, media, and religious activity, and regularly arrest, torture, and even kill dissenters with little or no legal due process.

Second-Generation Rights

The second generation of rights comprises social, economic, and cultural rights. These can be traced in part back to the labor and socialist reform movements of the nineteenth century. This was a time when many people, even in countries such as the United States and Great Britain that protected formal political rights, were desperately poor. People who were starving or homeless, reformers argued, had little use for freedom of the press or the right to vote.

As represented in Articles 22–26 of the UDHR, these rights include:

- The right to social security
- The right to adequate food, housing, and medical care
- The right to work/employment
- The right to join labor unions
- The right to equal pay for equal work
- The right to leisure and periodic holidays
- The right to basic education

Some of these rights are characterized as "positive rights." Unlike "negative rights," these rights may require actions by government to fulfill them. To enable individuals to enjoy the right to education may require the government to provide staffed schools. To ensure that people have adequate food and medical care may require government laws and spending programs.

Most stark examples of the failure to provide second-generation rights are from developing nations, such as those in Africa. Amnesty International, in its 2008 report, asserted that although many African countries enjoyed increased economic growth,

> millions of people continued to live without access to the basic requirements of a dignified life, such as adequate housing, education or health care. Political instability, armed conflict, corruption, underdevelopment and underinvestment in basic social services all contributed to the failure to make economic, social and cultural rights a reality for men, women and children across the region.[16]

But wealthy countries have also been criticized. Critics of America's health care system, for example, sometimes argue that the United States fails to provide health care access as a human right for its citizens.

Third-Generation Rights

Third-generation rights, sometimes called "solidarity rights," are rights that go beyond the individual rights of the first two generations. Although not as clearly outlined as first- and second-generation rights, in general they are collective rights that apply to whole populations of people rather than to individuals. These rights are sometimes traced to the ideas, aspirations, and demands of nations that did not exist in 1948 but were under European colonial rule. Third-generation rights (some of which are suggested in Articles 15 and 27 of the UDHR) include:

- The right to political, economic, and cultural self-determination
- The right to economic and social development
- The right to benefit from shared planetary resources, including scientific and technological advances
- The right to peace (freedom from war)

A prominent example of a collective right to self-determination is the case of Tibet, a province of China, but also a land and a people with centuries of history as a separate domain and a distinctive culture. The government of China has been accused of human rights violations in its treatment of the Tibetan people. Many of these accusations involve violations of individual human rights, such as imprisonment of political dissenters, restrictions on religious freedoms and practices, economic discrimination in policies that favor Chinese over Tibetans, and limits on free speech. However, the Chinese government has also been charged with violating the collective right of the Tibetan people to rule themselves according to their own traditions. Tibetan society features a special strain of Bud-

> " Tibetan activists and their foreign supporters have called not only for China to respect Tibetans' individual human rights but also for China to recognize Tibet's collective right to self-rule. "

dhism and has traditionally been dominated by Buddhist monks and ruled by the Dalai Lama, himself a monk. Tibetan activists and their foreign supporters have called not only for China to respect Tibetans' individual human rights but also for China to recognize Tibet's collective right to self-rule.

Past and Present Debates over Human Rights Categories

Since 1948 nations have argued that some human rights are more "real" than others. The United States, in championing human rights, has placed highest priority on political and civil rights. Social and economic rights, in U.S. government statements, are usually not called rights at all but instead are "aspirations"—goals that governments should aim for but not guarantee. Meanwhile, socialist and Communist nations such as China, Vietnam, and the (former) Soviet Union dismissed political and civil rights as something only the wealthy few were concerned about. Instead, they argued that the most important human rights involve basic material needs. A 1991 analysis by the Chinese government argued that, rather than political or civil rights, the abilities "to eat their fill and dress warmly were the fundamental demands of the Chinese people who had long suffered cold and hunger."[17] Meanwhile, many leaders of developing nations in Africa and Asia have argued that second-generation economic/social rights as well as national self-determination, economic development, and other third-generation rights should take priority over free speech and other first-generation rights.

> " A 1993 world conference on human rights held in Vienna, Austria, produced a consensus statement declaring human rights of all categories to be interdependent and interrelated. "

However, in recent years there has been a growing international consensus that debates over which rights are most important miss the point. Political and civil rights are hard to exercise and hold little meaning for a person who lacks basic food, water, medical care, and other material sustenance—a situation faced by billions of people in the world today. On the other hand, a functioning government that respects basic civil and legal rights does seem to be a necessity for sustainable national economic development that provides basic social, cultural, and economic rights to people. A 1993 world conference on human rights held in Vienna, Austria, produced a consensus statement declaring human rights of all categories to be interdependent and interrelated. This "means that civil and political, economic, social and cultural rights are interrelated and are co-equal in importance," argues Filipino human rights lawyer René V. Sarmiento. "They form an indivisible whole." Sarmiento and others maintain that only an equal emphasis on all human rights can ensure that humans can "live decently and in dignity."[18]

What Are Human Rights?

❝When human rights are confused with social or economic goals, human dignity is debased—and basic rights become more politically tenuous.❞

—Joseph Loconte, "The United Nations' Disarray," *Christianity Today*, February 1, 2007.

Loconte is a senior fellow at the Ethics and Public Policy Center and a distinguished visiting professor at Pepperdine University's School of Public Policy.

❝Civil and political rights and economic, social, and cultural rights are mutually reinforcing and derive from a single principle—the fundamental dignity of each human being.❞

—Joseph Amon, "Preventing the Further Spread of HIV/AIDS: The Essential Role of Human Rights," in *Human Rights Watch World Report 2006*. New York: Seven Stories, 2006.

Amon directs the HIV/AIDS Program at Human Rights Watch.

Bracketed quotes indicate conflicting positions.

* Editor's Note: While the definition of a primary source can be narrowly or broadly defined, for the purposes of Compact Research, a primary source consists of: 1) results of original research presented by an organization or researcher; 2) eyewitness accounts of events, personal experience, or work experience; 3) first-person editorials offering pundits' opinions; 4) government officials presenting political plans and/or policies; 5) representatives of organizations presenting testimony or policy.

66 Decent housing, good medical care and decent jobs are not rights at all, at least not in a free society—they're wishes. 99

—Walter Williams, "Rights v. Wishes, *Capitalism Magazine*, October 27, 2002. www.capmag.com.

Williams is a conservative author and syndicated columnist.

66 Political rights can be enjoyed only when basic human needs have been satisfied. Without economic security, freedom of conscience—the liberty to grow as an individual—is impossible. 99

—Jason Mark, "At the Millennium, a Broader Vision of Human Rights," January 2001. www.globalexchange.org.

Mark is a human rights activist with Global Exchange.

66 Human rights require three interlocking qualities: rights must be *natural* (inherent in human beings), *equal* (the same for everyone) and *universal* (applicable everywhere). 99

—Lynn Hunt, *Inventing Human Rights: A History*. New York: Norton, 2007.

Hunt is a professor of history at the University of California at Los Angeles.

66 The Universal Declaration and its core values—inherent human dignity, justice, non-discrimination, equality, fairness and universality—apply to everyone, everywhere, always. 99

—Louise Arbor, statement on Human Rights Day, December 10, 2007.

Arbor served as UN High Commissioner for Human Rights from 2004 to 2008.

> **Human rights are basic rights and freedoms that all people are entitled to regardless of nationality, sex, national or ethnic origin, race, religion, language, or other status.**

—Amnesty International, "Human Rights," 2008. www.amnestyusa.org.

Amnesty International is one of the world's largest independent human rights groups.

> **[Human rights] should not be a North-South issue. . . . Many southern governments today are strong defenders of human rights, and . . . some northern governments are major human rights problems.**

—Kenneth Roth, "UN Reform Agenda and Human Rights," in *Irrelevant or Indispensable? The United Nations at the 21st Century*, Paul Heinbecker and Patricia Goff, eds. Waterloo, ON: Wilfrid Laurier, 2005.

Roth is executive director of Human Rights Watch, an U.S.-based international human rights organization that investigates human rights conditions in more than 70 countries.

> **[The Cairo Declaration of Human Rights in Islam] is not an alternative, competing worldview on human rights. It complements the Universal Declaration as it addresses religious and cultural specificity of the Muslim countries.**

—Abdullah Hussain Haroon, quoted in "The Cairo Declaration and the Universality of Human Rights," jointly written statement of the International Humanist and Ethical Union, the Association for World Education, and the Association of World Citizens, March 4, 2008.

Haroon is the Pakistani ambassador to the United Nations.

> **The Cairo Declaration of Human Rights in Islam is clearly an attempt to limit the rights enshrined in the UDHR and the International Covenants. It can in no sense be seen as complementary to the Universal Declaration.**

—"The Cairo Declaration and the Universality of Human Rights," joint written statement of the International Humanist and Ethical Union, the Association for World Education, and the Association of World Citizens, March 4, 2008.

The three groups are nongovernmental organizations with consultative status at the United Nations.

Facts and Illustrations

What Are Human Rights?

- The Universal Declaration of Human Rights consists of a preamble and **30 articles** defining different rights.

- Prior to adopting the Universal Declaration on Human Rights, the Third Committee (a committee within the UN General Assembly) held **85 meetings** and more than **1,400 separate votes** on the draft document.

- The **UN General Assembly** adopted the UDHR on December 10, 1948, by a vote of 48-0, with 8 countries abstaining.

- The UDHR has been translated into more than **300 languages**.

- Parts of the Universal Declaration of Human Rights have been **directly incorporated into the constitutions of nations**, including El Salvador, Haiti, Indonesia, Jordan, and Syria.

- In 2002, at a UN-sponsored food summit, the United States was the **only nation out of 182** that opposed all references to food as a human right in the summit's declaration.

- December 10, 2008, marked the sixtieth anniversary of the **Universal Declaration of Human Rights**.

What Americans Think Should Be a Human Right

A 2007 poll by the Opportunity Agenda asked Americans about a number of issues relating to human rights. The results show what percentage of people strongly agreed that the issue should be a human right. Equality and nondiscrimination were among the top issues Americans strongly believed should be human rights.

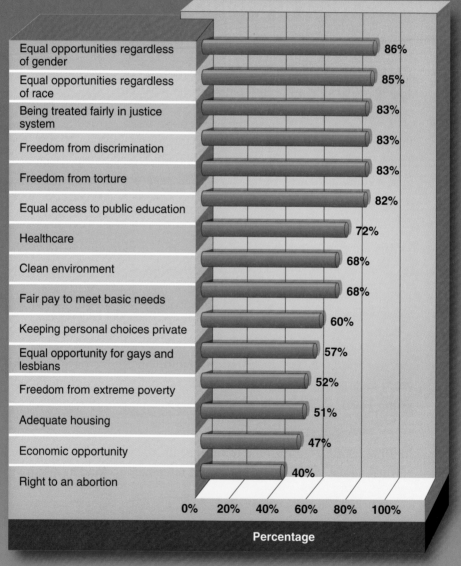

Issue	Percentage
Equal opportunities regardless of gender	86%
Equal opportunities regardless of race	85%
Being treated fairly in justice system	83%
Freedom from discrimination	83%
Freedom from torture	83%
Equal access to public education	82%
Healthcare	72%
Clean environment	68%
Fair pay to meet basic needs	68%
Keeping personal choices private	60%
Equal opportunity for gays and lesbians	57%
Freedom from extreme poverty	52%
Adequate housing	51%
Economic opportunity	47%
Right to an abortion	40%

Percentage

Source: The Opportunity Agenda, "New Report by Opportunity Agenda Shows Americans Are Concerned About Human Rights at Home," December 2007. www.opportunityagenda.org.

Most Americans Think Everyone Should Have Basic Human Rights

A 2007 human rights survey showed that most Americans believe that everyone should have basic human rights and that those rights should not be dictated by the government.

"Do you believe that every person has basic rights that are common to all human beings, regardless of whether their government recognizes those rights or not; OR do you believe that rights are given to an individual by his or her government? Do you feel that way strongly or somewhat?"

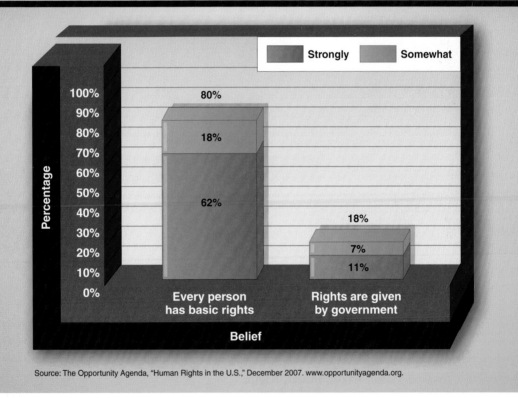

Source: The Opportunity Agenda, "Human Rights in the U.S.," December 2007. www.opportunityagenda.org.

- Amnesty International reports that **840 million** people are chronically malnourished and that more than **100 million children** do not have access to basic primary education.

Many Nations Still Not Considered Free

According to Freedom House, a nonprofit organization that surveys the state of civil liberties, political rights, economic freedom, and human rights around the world, many countries are still ranked as "Not Free" or only "Partly Free."

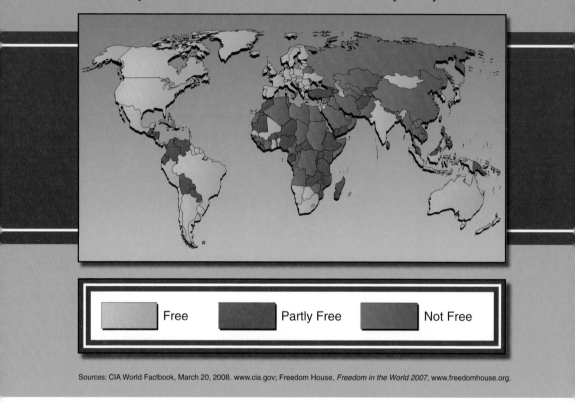

Free   Partly Free   Not Free

Sources: CIA World Factbook, March 20, 2008. www.cia.gov; Freedom House, *Freedom in the World 2007*, www.freedomhouse.org.

- According to a Gallup poll, when Americans were asked what they admired least about the Muslim world, **6 percent** said inadequate protection of human rights.

- **Eleanor Roosevelt** was a key contributor to the drafting of the Universal Declaration of Human Rights.

law and and have little real impact on human rights.

The UN Security Council is both more powerful and less [...]tive than the General Assembly, having five permanent and t[...] members. It is charged by the UN charter with primary respon[...] maintaining international peace and security. Unlike the Gene[...]bly, the Security Council has authority to impose economi[...] and military force to enforce international laws and UN res[...] successful past example of such Security Council action was a 1977 imposition of a mandatory arms embargo against South Africa that lasted until its white-supremacist apartheid system was ended in the 1990s.

More recently, the Security Council has held debates over the situation in Myanmar (Burma) and whether its military government should be required to release political prisoners, including Aung San Suu Kyi (winner of 1990 elections held in Myanmar and the 1991 Nobel Peace Prize recipient), cease attacks [...] minorities, and work with the United Nations to restore democ[...] ernment. In October 2007 the council issued a formal censure [...] mar that stated it "strongly deplores" violent crackdowns agains[...] protesters in August/September street demonstrations and call[...] release of political prisoners.

The five permanent members—China, Russia, Great Britai[...] and the United States—have veto power on any resolution. Th[...] ues to be a significant barrier to effective UN action, critics [...] because a single nation can stop significant economic sanction[...] tary actions. In the case of Myanmar, a resolution requiring t[...] of political prisoners and a speedy transition to democracy won[...] support in the Security Council in a January 2007 vote but w[...] by China and Russia.

In addition to the two voting bodies described above, the [...] numerous other suborganizations that execute UN policies [...] with various international problems. The secretary-general of th[...]

> Since 194[...]
> United Na[...]
> has negot[...]
> and adopt[...]
> merous de[...]
> tions and [...]
> tions deal[...]
> human rig[...]

How Can Global Human Rights Best Be Protected?

> "The protection of human rights, alongside peace and security, and economic and social development has been one of the three pillars of the UN's work since its creation."
>
> —Amnesty International, "The United Nations."

> "The UN's ethos of cooperation and multiculturalism, though useful in other contexts, is completely incompatible with the goal of exposing human rights abusers and protecting innocent people."
>
> —Joseph Loconte, testimony before the U.S. House of Representatives Committee on International Relations.

Defining human rights and establishing universal standards for them has been a central goal of the United Nations and international human rights law, beginning with the 1948 creation of the Universal Declaration of Human Rights. However, such standardization does not by itself ensure that human rights are actually upheld. The challenge of protecting human rights is one faced by both national governments and international institutions, including the United Nations.

The primary responsibility of human rights protection remains lodged in the governments of sovereign nations. Many governments have human rights provisions in their laws or constitutions (America's Bill of

Rights is one of the oldest examples). In most nations the
including courts and (presumably) independent judges, t
in holding government leaders accountable for human righ
Some nations, including Australia and Canada, have also est
cial bureaus or independent commissions that monitor and r
rights abuses. However, the fact that national government
sible for policing their own human rights actions strikes m
as problematic. "Governments are the last organization to
the field of human rights," writes author Gil Loescher. "Eve
pledge themselves to be its protectors, they are the chief off

The United Nations

Dealing with problems that nations by themselves cannot
primary reason the United Nations was founded in 1945.
has been at the epicenter of the modern global human rights
Its charter places the promotion and protection of human rig
its main purposes. But its effectiveness remains open to deba
complicated by the fact that the UN is not a monolithic orga
rather a complex network of organizations, agencies, and aff

The General Assembly and the Security Council are th
legislative bodies of the United Nations. The General Assemb
all member states are represented and are granted one vote, h
passes UN resolutions, and approves UN declarations and

> **The primary responsibility of human rights protection remains lodged in the governments of sovereign nations.**

2007, for example
General Assembly vo
of a universal mora
the death penalty an
a Declaration on the
Indigenous Peoples.
argued the human r
nization Amnesty I
al, "showed exactly t
direction the world
the UN: states insp

other to better performance, rather than running each other d
lowest common denominator. This was the UN at its best."20
others maintain that such UN votes do not create binding in

Facts and Illustrations

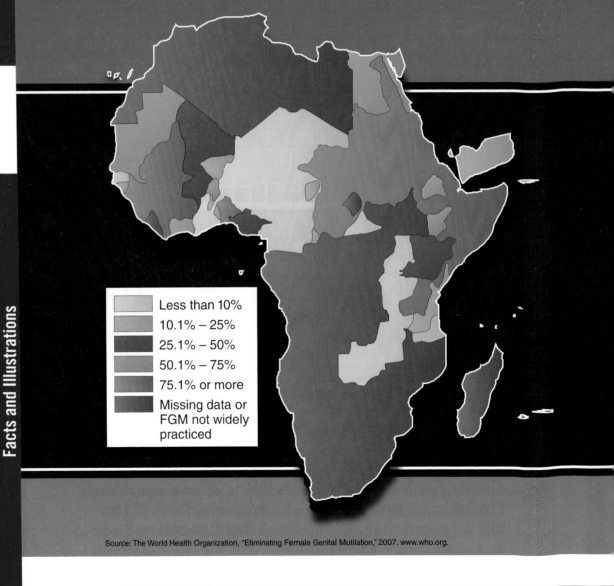

Female Genital Mutilation

The World Health Organization estimates that between 100 million and 140 million girls and women alive today have experienced some form of female genital mutilation (FGM), a forced, painful procedure that renders a woman's genitals severely scarred and incapable of sensation. The majority of mutilations, 88.5 percent, happened in Muslim nations. The map shows the areas where FGM is practiced. Because the practice can vary even within one country no national borders are shown.

Less than 10%
10.1% – 25%
25.1% – 50%
50.1% – 75%
75.1% or more
Missing data or FGM not widely practiced

Source: The World Health Organization, "Eliminating Female Genital Mutilation," 2007. www.who.org.

law and and have little real impact on human rights.

The UN Security Council is both more powerful and less representative than the General Assembly, having five permanent and ten rotating members. It is charged by the UN charter with primary responsibility for maintaining international peace and security. Unlike the General Assembly, the Security Council has authority to impose economic sanctions and military force to enforce international laws and UN resolutions. A successful past example of such Security Council action was a 1977 imposition of a mandatory arms embargo against South Africa that lasted until its white-supremacist apartheid system was ended in the 1990s.

More recently, the Security Council has held debates over the situation in Myanmar (Burma) and whether its military government should be required to release political prisoners, including Aung San Suu Kyi (winner of 1990 elections held in Myanmar and the 1991 Nobel Peace Prize recipient), cease attacks on ethnic minorities, and work with the United Nations to restore democratic government. In October 2007 the council issued a formal censure of Myanmar that stated it "strongly deplores" violent crackdowns against peaceful protesters in August/September street demonstrations and called for the release of political prisoners.

> " Since 1945 the United Nations has negotiated and adopted numerous declarations and conventions dealing with human rights. "

The five permanent members—China, Russia, Great Britain, France, and the United States—have veto power on any resolution. This continues to be a significant barrier to effective UN action, critics contend, because a single nation can stop significant economic sanctions or military actions. In the case of Myanmar, a resolution requiring the release of political prisoners and a speedy transition to democracy won majority support in the Security Council in a January 2007 vote but was vetoed by China and Russia.

In addition to the two voting bodies described above, the UN has numerous other suborganizations that execute UN policies and deal with various international problems. The secretary-general of the United

Nations is the executive head of these various organizations, one of which is the Office of the High Commissioner for Human Rights, created in 1993. The commissioner's duties include providing technical advice and financial assistance in the field of human rights to states that request such aid, coordinating human rights promotion and protection activities of the various UN agencies and programs, and educating the general public on human rights.

UN Treaties

The primary legal instruments the UN has used to promote and uphold human rights has been international treaties. Since 1945 the United Nations has negotiated and adopted numerous declarations and con-ventions dealing with human rights. Declarations such as the UDHR refer to formal statements of agreement. They are not legally enforce-able. Conventions (also called covenants) are written agreements that are officially binding on states that ratify them. Ratifying countries are supposed to honor such commitments when making and enforcing their domestic laws. Each UN convention also usually creates its own treaty body—a special UN committee that oversees international enforcement of that particular treaty. Ratifying states are supposed to submit peri-odic reports to these committees on their progress in implementing the treaty in question. The committees can receive complaints or allegations of problems, discuss remedies, and make recommendations. They some-times appoint independent experts (called special rapporteurs) who visit countries, investigate particular human rights concerns, and report back to the treaty body.

The Human Rights Council and the Human Rights Commission

In addition to the specific treaty bodies, the United Nations has a special-ized committee on human rights. From 1946 to 2006 this was the UN Commission on Human Rights. Consisting of diplomats representing 53 countries, it was responsible for negotiating and submitting treaties to the General Assembly for vote and recommendations to the Security Council for action. In the 1960s and 1970s the commission expanded its duties to include responding to complaints about human rights abuses and investigating human rights problems.

However, the commission was often criticized for not being effective. It met only once a year for a few weeks. Its investigative work was done behind closed doors and only with the consent of the investigated country. In addition, many of the nations that participated in the commission had notably bad human rights records themselves. For some critics, the last straw was when Sudan joined in 2004, even though, as former Republican congressional leader Newt Gingrich noted, "its Islamist dictatorship is accused of murdering thousands of Africans, fostering a starvation policy that could kill a million more . . . and . . . has been responsible for what Secretary General Kofi Annan says is the biggest humanitarian crisis on the planet."[21] Gingrich and others believed that nations such as Sudan joined the commission with the purpose of deflecting human rights criticisms from themselves and blocking effective UN action. According to conservative ethics scholar Joseph Loconte, many "attempts to produce resolutions critical of human-rights violators routinely died in their crib—blocked in backroom maneuvers."[22] As a result, most public human rights criticisms produced by the commission were directed at only a few countries.

> " Each UN convention also usually creates its own treaty body—a special UN committee that oversees international enforcement of that particular treaty. "

In March 2006 the UN General Assembly voted to replace the commission with the Human Rights Council. The new HRC held its first meetings in June 2006. It had responsibilities similar to its predecessor but, unlike the commission, would meet several times throughout the year, issue regular reports on the human rights records of all UN members, and would have the power to remove noncompliant members. Since 2006 the HRC has heard reports on Myanmar and forwarded recommended actions to the Security Council, adopted a reform that would enable individuals to petition the UN about violations of their economic, social, and cultural rights, and debated how its independent human rights experts should be chosen. However, some critics of the Human Rights Council argue that its record (especially its focus on Israel to the exclusion of other countries) is not much better than the commission it replaced. This may be in part because, like its predecessor, its membership has included many nations, such as Azerbaijan, Cuba, Pakistan, China, Nigeria, and Saudi Arabia, with poor human rights records.

> **Nongovernmental organizations (NGOs) have historically played an important role in promoting and protecting international human rights.**

Journalist James Traub has argued that the UN is only as strong as its weakest member-states in enforcing human rights. He notes that more than half the members of the new council come from Africa and Asia, "where very few nations conformed to the principles of the Universal Declaration of Human Rights. And even the democracies among them were loath to meddle in the affairs of others and were inclined to view human rights as a club wielded by the West. Perhaps the UN was simply not suited to this line of work."[23]

Regional Bodies

In addition to the United Nations itself, other international organizations work to promote and protect human rights at the regional level. Western European countries agreed to their own human rights treaty (the European Convention for the Protection of Human Rights and Fundamental Freedoms) that was similar to the UDHR but included enforcement measures. A European Court of Human Rights was created to interpret the convention, take in complaints, and issue rulings. The Organization of American States (OAS), a regional group of governments covering North and South America, formally adopted its own human rights treaty (the American Convention on Human Rights) in 1969. Two organizations enforce the human rights listed in that convention: The Inter-American Commission on Human Rights and the Inter-American Court of Human Rights. In Africa, the Organization of African Unity (OAU) adopted the African Charter on Human and People's Rights in 1981. A later protocol to the African charter authorized a human rights court that as of 2008 had yet to begin operations. Other regions of the world, including the Middle East and Asia, have not yet developed fully functioning regional systems for promoting and protecting human rights.

Private Organizations

Private organizations, sometimes called nongovernmental organizations (NGOs), have historically played an important role in promoting and protecting international human rights. They include well-known human rights groups, such as Amnesty International and Human Rights Watch, religious and charitable organizations, community associations, and citizens groups. Among the things NGOs do is monitor human rights abuses and report their results to UN bodies and/or to the general public, provide legal counsel and other assistance to human rights victims and local human rights activists, lobby governments to sign and ratify human rights treaties, and educate local government officials about how to uphold them.

The long-term effectiveness of such groups, working with the international structure of the United Nations, remains in question. While the various human rights NGOs and UN bodies have done significant work and employ thousands of people to uphold human rights, the basic fact remains that the United Nations since its inception was simply not designed or meant to function as a world police force. As a practical matter, the UN has little or no independent law enforcement powers over sovereign nations. Much of what is done in human rights work, both on the international and local levels, aims at shaming, cajoling, or otherwise persuading heads of state and other national government officials to take action. The effectiveness of the UN and similar intergovernmental organizations must be judged with this in mind.

How Can Global Human Rights Best Be Protected?

> **The Universal Declaration . . . mapped out the international human rights agenda, established the benchmark for state conduct, inspired provisions in many national laws and international conventions, and led to the creation of long-term national infrastructures for the protection and promotion of human rights.**

—International Commission on Intervention and State Sovereignty, *Responsibility to Protect: Report of the International Commission on Intervention and State Sovereignty*, December 2001.

The International Commission on Intervention and State Sovereignty was a special UN-sponsored study group that analyzed and reported on how and when the international community should intervene in the affairs of nations to protect human rights.

> **But the fundamental freedoms enshrined in [the Universal Declaration of Human Rights] are still not a reality for everyone. Too often, Governments lack the political will to implement international norms they have willingly accepted.**

—Ban Ki-moon, statement on Human Rights Day, December 10, 2007. www.un.org.

Ki-moon is secretary-general of the United Nations.

Bracketed quotes indicate conflicting positions.

* Editor's Note: While the definition of a primary source can be narrowly or broadly defined, for the purposes of Compact Research, a primary source consists of: 1) results of original research presented by an organization or researcher; 2) eyewitness accounts of events, personal experience, or work experience; 3) first-person editorials offering pundits' opinions; 4) government officials presenting political plans and/or policies; 5) representatives of organizations presenting testimony or policy.

> 66 It remains difficult for the United Nations or outside forces to act without the backing of major powers and the consent of the territorial government. It is obvious that countries such as Russia and China are too strong to challenge, however reprehensible their behavior be with respect to human rights. 99

—Richard A. Falk, in Roger Normand and Sarah Zaidi, *Human Rights at the UN: The Political History of Universal Justice.* Bloomington: Indiana University Press, 2007.

Falk, a retired professor of international relations at Princeton University, is an author and UN consulting expert on human rights issues.

> 66 Domestic interest groups with ties to the international community can be particularly effective in pressuring governments to abide by universal human rights standards. 99

—Jerry Pubantz. "Constructing Reason: Human Rights and the Democratization of the United Nations," *Social Forces,* December 2005.

Pubantz is a political science professor at the University of North Carolina at Greensboro.

> 66 Even the most repressive regimes want to look nice. 99

—Newton R. Bowles, *The Diplomacy of Hope: The United Nations Since the Cold War.* New York: I.B. Tauris, 2004.

Bowles is a Canadian diplomat who has worked for the United Nations in various capacities since 1945.

> 66 The United Nations has declared its desire to become a true world government with sweeping global authority, replacing the God-given rights that Americans have long enjoyed under our Declaration of Independence with the arbitrary state-conferred benefits of the UN's Universal Declaration of Human Rights. 99

—Nathan Tabor, *The Beast on the East River.* Nashville, TN: Nelson Current, 2006.

Tabor is a conservative columnist and radio commentator, and a member of the Council for National Policy.

Facts and Illustrations

How Can Global Human Rights Best Be Protected?

- The United Nations has **192** member nations.

- The United Nations has produced more than **80 conventions and declarations** related to human rights.

- Every UN member state has signed and ratified at least one major human rights treaty; **80 percent** of states have ratified at least four.

- In 2005 the UN Commission on Human Rights adopted eight resolutions **condemning specific states for human rights violations**. Israel was the subject of four resolutions, while Belarus, Myanmar (Burma), Cuba, and North Korea received one each.

- The Office of the High Commissioner for Human Rights, headquartered in Geneva, Switzerland, has a staff of roughly **1,000 people working in 50 countries** with a total annual budget of roughly $150 million.

- The number of nongovernmental organizations (NGOs) that officially consult with the UN has risen from 41 in 1948 to 377 in 1968 to 1,200 in 1997 to **2,600** in 2005.

- In 2008 Amnesty International had more than **2 million** members and supporters in more than 150 countries, organized into thousands of volunteer groups.

Top 20 Executors Worldwide

The use of the death penalty places the United States in the company of some of the worst human rights abusers in the world. Sixty-five percent of nations that most use the death penalty are Muslim. Other top executors include China, Vietnam, Japan, and the United States.

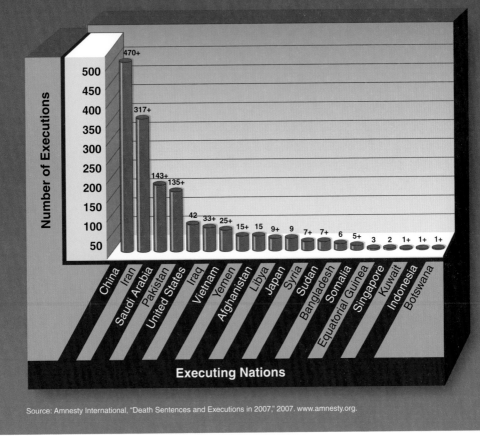

Source: Amnesty International, "Death Sentences and Executions in 2007," 2007. www.amnesty.org.

- In a recent Gallup poll Americans were asked how important promoting and defending human rights should be as a U.S. foreign policy goal; **86 percent** said it was important.

- According to Amnesty International's 2008 report on human rights, **81 countries still torture** or mistreat prisoners or detainees, **77 countries** still place restrictions on free speech, and **54 countries** still conduct grossly unfair criminal trials.

Female Genital Mutilation

The World Health Organization estimates that between 100 million and 140 million girls and women alive today have experienced some form of female genital mutilation (FGM), a forced, painful procedure that renders a woman's genitals severely scarred and incapable of sensation. The majority of mutilations, 88.5 percent, happened in Muslim nations. The map shows the areas where FGM is practiced. Because the practice can vary even within one country no national borders are shown.

Less than 10%
10.1% – 25%
25.1% – 50%
50.1% – 75%
75.1% or more
Missing data or FGM not widely practiced

Source: The World Health Organization, "Eliminating Female Genital Mutilation," 2007. www.who.org.

U.S. Assistance to Iraqi Refugees Growing

Due to the war in Iraq, the United States has aided in the relocation and support of thousands of Iraqi refugees. In 2008 (through September 12) more than 12,000 Iraqis were admitted to the United States as refugees. In 2008 the United States spent more than $318 million on aid for the refugees, conflict victims, and internationally displaced people. From 2003–2008 the United States was the biggest contributor to Iraqi programs providing food, health care, education, water and sanitation, and emergency shelter and protection.

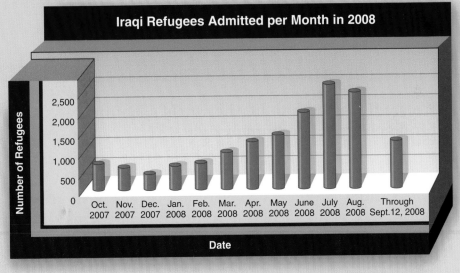

Iraqi Refugees Admitted per Month in 2008

Source: U.S. Department of State, "U.S. Surpasses Goal of Admitting 12,000 Iraqi Refugees in Fiscal Year 2008; Assistance Reaches New Heights," September 12, 2008. www.state.gov.

- In a PIPA-CCFR poll **66 percent** of Americans favored giving developmental aid to help nations promote new democracies and thus human rights.

- According to a poll from the Opportunity Agenda, **75 percent** of Americans believe the United States should focus on making regular progress on human rights, and **80 percent** say that "every person has basic human rights regardless of whether their government recognizes those rights or not."

Should U.S. Foreign Policy Consider Human Rights?

"We shall continue to be the world's leading advocate for democracy and human rights."

—Undersecretary of State Paula Dobriansky, comments to the Senate Foreign Relations Committee.

"The United States . . . pretends to support universal human rights when actually it recognizes different standards for itself and its friends than those it applies to its enemies."

—Julie A. Mertus, *Bait and Switch: Human Rights and U.S. Foreign Policy.*

Although America has a long history of celebrating liberty and other rights dating back to its founding, U.S. foreign policy did not make human rights a high-profile issue until the 1970s. This was a time when many Americans were becoming dismayed by the Vietnam War and by reports that the United States was allied with or actively supporting repressive governments. In 1975 Congress modified federal law on foreign aid to tie it more closely to a country's human rights record. Congress also mandated that the State Department issue annual reports on the human rights performances of nations.

These changes were at first resisted by the State Department but gained a new champion in the White House with President Jimmy

Carter's election to the presidency in 1976. "Our moral sense," Carter asserted in his 1977 inaugural address, "dictates a clear-cut preference for those societies which share with us an abiding respect for individual human rights."[24] In a later speech before human rights workers and members of Congress, he went on to argue that "human rights is the soul of foreign policy—because human rights is the very soul of our sense of nationhood."[25] Carter argued moreover that U.S. security would be enhanced if more countries respected human rights, that America had legal obligations and responsibilities to promote human rights, and that such promotion could be done without damage to other American political, economic, and military interests. Carter's emphasis on human rights was one of the president's lasting achievements. All presidents since then have to various degrees continued to make human rights promotion a goal of foreign policy. The Bureau of Democracy, Human Rights, and Labor (DRL) is the office within the U.S. State Department that handles human rights.

> '' 'Our moral sense,' Carter asserted in his 1977 inaugural address, 'dictates a clear-cut preference for those societies which share with us an abiding respect for individual human rights.' ''

Diplomatic Tools to Promote Human Rights

The United States uses various diplomatic tools and programs to promote global human rights. These include:

- Private diplomatic exchanges with foreign leaders and officials.
- Prominent public statements meant to put foreign governments on notice and to raise hopes among human rights activists and dissidents. In 2007, for example, President George W. Bush publicly criticized the Russian government for arresting people who took part in public demonstrations on the eve of elections, and called on that government to honor freedoms of expression and assembly: "I am particularly troubled by the use of force . . . to stop these peaceful activities and to prevent some journalists and human rights activists from covering them."[26]

- Symbolic gestures, such as a reduction in military or diplomatic contacts, or hosting political dissidents or human rights activists. An example is George W. Bush presenting a medal to the Dalai Lama in 2007 as a way of symbolically expressing concern about Chinese human rights violations in Tibet.
- Positive measures, such as monetary grants to help countries build institutions in support of human rights, or presidential visits to nations in recognition of an improved human rights record.
- Sanctions, such as reductions in military sales or economic ties. In the 1980s economic sanctions against South Africa helped to bring about the release of political prisoner Nelson Mandela and the eventual end of the South African apartheid regime.

Several recent federal laws and programs have asserted the priority of human rights in American foreign policy. The International Religious Freedom Act, passed by Congress in 1998, officially makes the promotion of religious freedom a basic aim of U.S. foreign policy. It mandates annual State Department reports on the status of religious freedom in all foreign countries and requires the U.S. president to consider various diplomatic options, including withholding non-humanitarian aid, when a country is flagged for persecuting religious minorities. The Human Rights Development Fund (HDRF), also begun in 1998, is money that the DRL can award to projects and organizations seeking to promote democratic development and human rights. It has grown from $7.8 million in 1998 to almost $70 million in 2007.

Human Rights and Saudi Arabia

However, it is not too difficult to find places and instances in which human rights seem to play a minor role in America's dealings with other nations. American policy in Saudi Arabia is one example of how other foreign policy priorities have trumped human rights concerns.

Saudi Arabia is a monarchy in the Middle East with a population of almost 25 million. With a legal system based on Islamic law, with all religions other than the official state version of Sunni Islam practically outlawed, and with political power concentrated in the monarchy, Saudi Arabia is regarded by most observers as having a very poor human rights record. The U.S. State Department in its annual human rights report for 2007 took note of the following problems:

no right to peacefully change the government; infliction of severe pain by judicially sanctioned corporal punishments; beatings and other abuse; arbitrary arrest and detention, sometimes incommunicado; denial of fair public trials; political prisoners; exemption for the rule of law for some individuals and lack of judicial independence; restrictions on civil liberties such as the freedoms of speech, including the Internet, assembly, association, movement, and religion; corruption and lack of government transparency. Violence against women and discrimination on the basis of gender, religion, sect, and ethnicity were common.[27]

However, Saudi Arabia also possesses the world's largest known petroleum reserves and exports more than 1 million barrels of oil per day to the United States. The U.S. State Department has declared that "the continued availability of reliable sources of oil, particularly from Saudi Arabia, remains important to the prosperity of the United States." Saudi Arabia's position as one of the leaders of the Arab world, and its shared goals with the United States on maintaining Middle East stability and preventing terrorist attacks in both nations, have resulted in "close consultations" between the two countries "on international, economic, and development interest issues such as the Middle East peace process."[28]

The State Department goes on to say that "despite close cooperation on security issues, the United States remains concerned about human rights conditions in Saudi Arabia."[29] However, the United States has done relatively little to press human rights issues on the Saudi monarchy. For example,

> " In 2007 . . . President George W. Bush publicly criticized the Russian government for arresting people who took part in public demonstrations on the eve of elections, and called on that government to honor freedoms of expression and assembly. "

Saudi Arabia has been listed as a "country of particular concern" in the State Department's annual reports required under the 1998 International Religious Freedom Act. However, Bush made and later extended a special waiver exempting the U.S. government, for reasons of national security, from having to impose sanctions or otherwise confront Saudi Arabia about its poor religious freedom record.

> "It is not too difficult to find places and instances in which human rights seem to play a minor role in America's dealings with other nations."

American policies in Saudi Arabia and other places have led some to question America's commitment to human rights. The United States "has employed human rights selectively," argues foreign policy scholar Julie A. Mertus, "condemning the human rights abuses of its enemies while overlooking those of its allies."[30] But defenders of U.S. policies generally respond that American leaders must place the interests and concerns of the United States first and that although promoting human rights in other countries is important, it may sometimes need to be set aside to achieve other foreign policy goals.

Human Rights and the War on Terror

The 2001 terrorist attacks had a profound impact on U.S. foreign policy and the debate over human rights. The George W. Bush administration responded by tightening security measures and by stating that the nation was in an unofficial "war on terror"—a war with no obvious endpoint or boundary.

Part of the war on terror has been U.S.-led military actions against two nations—Afghanistan and Iraq. Afghanistan's government had permitted al Qaeda, a terrorist group responsible for planning and carrying out numerous terrorist acts, including the September 11 attacks, to set up camps and bases. The United States led a military invasion that toppled Afghanistan's government in late 2001. Iraq was accused by the Bush administration of cooperating with terrorists (not al Qaeda) and secretly and illegally developing weapons of mass destruction (chemical, biological, and nuclear weapons) that might possibly be used in a terrorist attack even larger than what happened on September 11. To prevent such a catastrophe, Bush ordered a U.S.-led military invasion that removed the Iraqi government in 2003. In both Afghanistan and Iraq thousands of U.S. troops remained to fight insurgents.

During both wars and subsequent occupations, the U.S. military captured people suspected of terrorist acts and took them to America's naval base in Guantánamo Bay, Cuba, as well as to secret facilities in other parts of the world. These detainees, deemed enemy combatants rather than prisoners of war (POWs have more rights under international law), have been held for years without being charged with specific crimes and without access to courts or lawyers. Their treatment has been at the center of controversy over whether the United States is honoring its human rights commitments.

The United States and Torture

The most serious charges against the United States are about torture and inhumane treatment. The United States is a ratifying member of the UN Convention Against Torture, which bans all torture and degrading treatment of people. However, there have been documented instances of the U.S. government secretly transferring terrorist suspects to other nations with the understanding that they may be interrogated in ways that amount to torture. Americans have been accused of engaging in torture themselves as well, despite official denials by Bush and others. Critics argue that Bush administration officials engaged in a process of defining and parsing the U.S. Constitution, the UN Convention Against Torture, and federal laws. The aim, critics say, was to narrowly define torture and permit what have been described as "enhanced interrogation techniques" on detainees. These techniques include waterboarding (controlled drowning) and other

> " There have been documented instances of the U.S. government secretly transferring terrorist suspects to other nations with the understanding that they may be interrogated in ways that amount to torture. "

methods that have in the past been commonly understood as torture.

The questions about America's human rights record have had an effect on foreign policy and human rights around the world. Many people have argued that the United States has lost much of its moral standing in criticizing other countries for human rights violations. Others have asserted that U.S. policies have encouraged other countries to use terrorism as an all-purpose excuse for their own human rights crackdowns. During a 2005 meeting between Egyptian prime minister Ahmed Nazif and representatives of Human Rights Watch, Nazif responded to allegations of torture by his security forces by stating, "We're just doing what the United States does."[31]

Defense of U.S. Actions Against Terrorist Suspects

Defenders of U.S. actions argue that terrorist suspects in Guantánamo and elsewhere are treated humanely, with good food, medical care, and religious freedom. Jack Goldsmith, an assistant attorney general from 2003 to 2004, argues that members of al Qaeda seek to gain political advantage by making false accusations of torture and other violations "as we now know al Qaeda training manuals advise them to do."[32]

But others have responded to accusations of torture and other human rights violations by defending them as regrettable but necessary for America's security. One argument is that terrorists under American detention may have information that can help authorities prevent another massive terrorist attack. "Getting at the information [detained terrorist suspects] possess could allow us to thwart major attacks, unravel their organization, and save thousands of lives," writes author and military analyst Mark Bowden. "They and their situation pose one of the strongest arguments in modern times for the use of torture."[33] Whether a hard-and-fast rule against torture, and other commitments to internationally defined human rights, is the best posture for U.S. foreign policy in its war on terror is something that continues to be debated.

Primary Source Quotes*

Should U.S. Foreign Policy Consider Human Rights?

66 **Promoting human rights and democracy is a cornerstone of American foreign policy. The Department of State integrates democracy and human rights promotion into all aspects of U.S. foreign policy by supporting freedom-loving people around the world in their efforts to protect human rights.** 99

—U.S. State Department Bureau of Public Affairs, *Human Rights: A Cornerstone of U.S. Foreign Policy*, December 8, 2005.

The Department of State, part of the executive branch of America's government, conducts and administers American foreign policy.

66 **The Bush administration's methodical disregard for the human rights of those detained in the campaign against terrorism has been disastrous for the global human rights cause.** 99

—Human Rights Watch, "Human Rights Agenda for the New Administration," October 2008. www.hrw.org.

Human Rights Watch is dedicated to protecting the human rights of people around the world.

Bracketed quotes indicate conflicting positions.

* Editor's Note: While the definition of a primary source can be narrowly or broadly defined, for the purposes of Compact Research, a primary source consists of: 1) results of original research presented by an organization or researcher; 2) eyewitness accounts of events, personal experience, or work experience; 3) first-person editorials offering pundits' opinions; 4) government officials presenting political plans and/or policies; 5) representatives of organizations presenting testimony or policy.

❝No country in the world should view itself as the incarnation of human rights, and use human rights as a tool to interfere in affairs of and exert pressure on other countries and realize its own strategic interests. . . . [America's] arrogant critiques on the human rights of other countries are always accompanied by a deliberate ignoring of serious human rights problems on its own territory.❞

—Information Office of the State Council, "The Human Rights Record of the United States in 2007," March 13, 2008.

The State Council is the foreign policy apparatus of the government of the People's Republic of China.

❝America has human rights language without a human rights culture—the talk without the walk. . . . U.S. citizens are far too willing to tolerate their government's abridgement of international human rights standards.❞

—Julie A. Mertus, "Bait and Switch? Human Rights and U.S. Foreign Policy," *FPIF Policy Report*, Foreign Policy in Focus, March 2004.

Mertus is a scholar and author of several books on human rights, the United States, and the United Nations.

❝No matter what it costs us, no matter how it scares us, no matter how foolish it seems to a cynical world, America should stand up for human rights.❞

—Chris Satullo, "A Not-So-Glorious Fourth," *Philadelphia Inquirer*, July 1, 2008.

Satullo is a columnist for the *Philadelphia Inquirer*.

❝If you don't violate someone's human rights some of the time, you probably aren't doing your job.❞

—Anonymous official, quoted in Matthew Rothschild, "Bush's Dishonor," *Progressive*, vol. 68, no. 7, July 2004.

An anonymous American military official involved in the supervision of captured terrorist suspects made this statement to a reporter for the *Washington Post* in 2002.

"The United States of America does not torture. And that's important for people around the world to understand."

—George W. Bush, statement at press conference, November 29, 2005.

Bush served as U.S. president from 2001 to 2009.

....

"There's substantial evidence that the United States routinely and knowingly "outsources" the application of torture by transferring terrorism suspects to countries that frequently violate international human rights norms."

—Sangitha McKenzie Miller, "Extraordinary Rendition, Extraordinary Mistake," *FPIF Policy Report*, Foreign Policy in Focus, August 29, 2008.

Miller is a researcher for Citizens for Global Solutions.

....

"America speaks anew to the peoples of the world. All who live in tyranny and hopelessness can know that the United States will not ignore your oppression or excuse your oppressors. When you stand for your liberty, we will stand with you."

—George W. Bush, second inaugural address, January 21, 2005.

Bush served as president of the United States from 2001 to 2009.

....

"Democracy and human rights activists overseas now spurn U.S. support for fear they will be tainted by association with a larger American agenda."

—William F. Schulz, introduction to *The Future of Human Rights: US Policy for a New Era*. Philadelphia: University of Pennsylvania Press, 2008.

Schulz is executive director of Amnesty International USA and the author of several books on human rights.

....

66 Enemy combatants need not be accorded every privilege granted legitimate prisoners of war; but they must be treated as human beings. This means that, in addition to physical torture, wanton abuse of their religious faith is out of bounds. 99

—Andrew Sullivan, "The Abolition of Torture," *New Republic*, December 19, 2005.

Sullivan is a writer on politics and culture.

66 To build a better, freer world, we must first behave in ways that reflect the decency and aspirations of the American people. This means ending the practice of shipping away prisoners in the dead of night to be tortured in far-off countries, of detaining thousands without charge or trial, of maintaining a network of secret prisons to jail people beyond the reach of law. 99

—Barack Obama, "Renewing American Leadership," *Foreign Affairs*, July/August 2007.

Obama was elected president of the United States in 2008.

Facts and Illustrations

Should U.S. Foreign Policy Consider Human Rights?

- The Bureau of Democracy, Human Rights, and Labor (DRL) in fiscal year 2007 administered **$340 million** from the Human Rights Development Fund and other appropriations. The money supported 200 programs in 50 countries advancing democracy and human rights.

- **$207 million** of the $340 million spent by DRL to promote human rights **was designated for one country—Iraq**.

- The U.S. State Department has a special emergency fund of **$1.5 million** to provide timely assistance to human rights activists whose lives or safety have been threatened because of their work.

- The criminal justice system in Saudi Arabia allows for flogging, the **cutting off of hands** for thieves, and execution by **beheading**. According to Human Rights Watch, 147 decapitations were carried out in 2007.

- The United States is one of the only nations in the world **not to sign or ratify** the UN Convention on Children's Rights.

- Since 2001 an estimated **150 foreign detainees** have been rendered from U.S. custody to a foreign country known to torture prisoners, including Egypt, Syria, Saudi Arabia, Jordan, and Pakistan.

Promoting Human Rights Not a Top Priority for Americans

Ongoing polls by the Pew Research Center for People and the Press have tracked what Americans consider "top priorities" for international issues. While "promoting human rights" was not a top priority (only 25 percent felt it was a top priority in 2008), "protecting groups/nations threatened with genocide" did rank higher, as 36 percent of Americans considered it a top priority in 2008. Protecting the United States from terrorism ranked the highest.

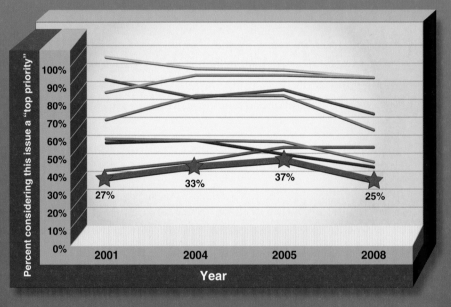

Protecting U.S. from terrorist attacks
Protecting American jobs
Preventing spread of weapons of mass destruction
Reducing spread of AIDS/other infectious diseases
Dealing with climate change
Protecting groups/nations threatened with genocide
Strengthening the UN
Promoting human rights

Source: Pew Research Center for People and the Press, "Declining Public Support for Global Engagement," September 24, 2008. http://people-press.org.

Americans Do Not Wish to Impose Human Rights on Other Countries

Americans polled in 2007 were asked if they agreed or disagreed with U.S. enforcement of human rights in other countries. A 64 percent majority did not think the United States should be involved.

Question: Do you agree that people in the United States should not try to interpret and enforce human rights for people living in other countries?

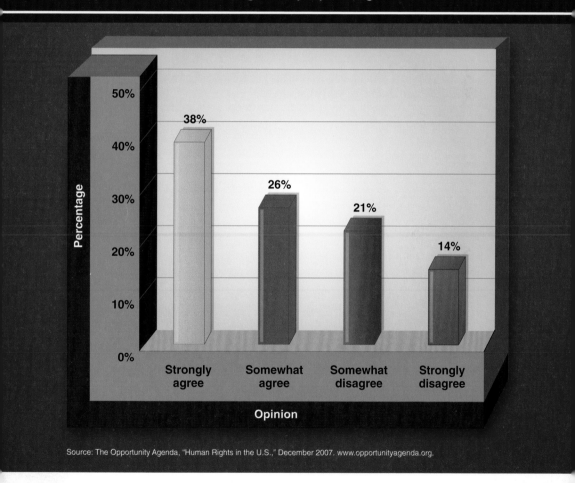

Source: The Opportunity Agenda, "Human Rights in the U.S.," December 2007. www.opportunityagenda.org.

- According to Amnesty International, there are estimated to be between **100 million** and **150 million** street children in the world, and the number is growing.

Public Opinion in Many Nations Opposes Torture

A 2008 survey of more than 19,000 people in 19 nations, including most of the world's largest countries, asked respondents whether they believed that all torture is immoral and should be prohibited, or whether the threat of terrorism justified torture if it could possibly save innocent lives. Those who justified torture in such circumstances were then asked whether governments should generally be allowed to torture. Among all nations, 57 percent favored a total ban, 26 percent an exception to save innocent lives, and 9 percent favored allowing government to use torture in general. The figures do not add up to 100 percent because some respondents did not know or state a position.

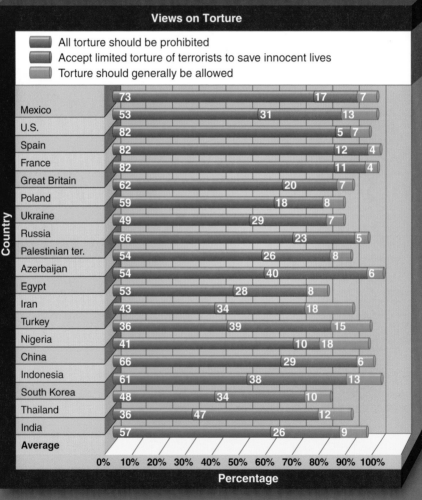

Views on Torture

Legend:
- All torture should be prohibited
- Accept limited torture of terrorists to save innocent lives
- Torture should generally be allowed

Country	All torture should be prohibited	Accept limited torture of terrorists to save innocent lives	Torture should generally be allowed
Mexico	73	17	7
U.S.	53	31	13
Spain	82	5	7
France	82	12	4
Great Britain	82	11	4
Poland	62	20	7
Ukraine	59	18	8
Russia	49	29	7
Palestinian ter.	66	23	5
Azerbaijan	54	26	8
Egypt	54	40	6
Iran	53	28	8
Turkey	43	34	18
Nigeria	36	39	15
China	41	10	18
Indonesia	66	29	6
South Korea	61	38	13
Thailand	48	34	10
India	36	47	12
Average	57	26	9

Percentage

Top 10 Human Rights Abusers

The 2007 report by the U.S. State Department singled out these 10 nations as the world's "most systematic human rights violators."

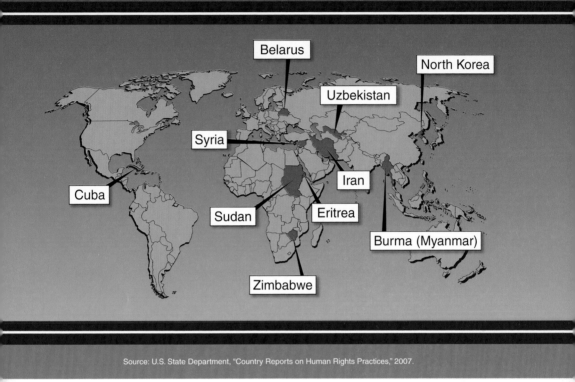

Source: U.S. State Department, "Country Reports on Human Rights Practices," 2007.

- As of August 2008 the U.S. military was holding **265 detainees** at Guantánamo Bay; more than 500 have been released or transferred to other countries.

- The U.S. government has confirmed that at least three terrorist suspects under U.S. custody have been subjected to **waterboarding**.

What Is the Future of Human Rights?

66In the face of numerous, pressing human rights crises, there is no shared vision among world leaders to address contemporary challenges of human rights in a world that is increasingly endangered, unsafe and unequal.99

—Amnesty International, *Amnesty International Report 2008.*

66The realization of human rights is never automatically achieved . . . [but] depends on the extent to which authorities and individuals take the human rights message to heart. In other words human rights are not a gift but a task for all of us.99

—Walter Kalin, *The Face of Human Rights.*

Sixty years after the Universal Declaration of Human Rights was adopted by the UN General Assembly, human rights have become a durable and popular concept around much of the world. The ideas found in the UDHR have become the basis for a significant body of international law. However, human rights have continued to be ignored in actual practice. From religious repression in China, political intimidation in elections in Zimbabwe, genocide in the Sudan, to human slave trafficking in many parts of the world, human rights violations continue to be a common occurrence. The persistence of human rights problems has caused some to raise questions about the future viability of the human rights ideal. "Viewed through the lens of gross violations by state and nonstate actors of every stripe," argue authors and activists Roger Normand and Sarah Zaidi, "it is tempting to conclude that the human rights idea has failed."[34]

In examining the future of human rights, several distinct trends can be noted. These include renewed debates over international military intervention to prevent or stop gross human rights abuses, new institutional efforts to hold international human rights violators legally accountable for their actions, and attempts to incorporate human rights ideas within other social movements confronting broad problems related to globalization and global poverty.

The Responsibility to Protect

In the late twentieth and early twenty-first centuries some of the greatest human rights problems have been not the product of repressive governments but of failed states and social breakdown related to civil war and ethnic conflict. In some cases, government armed forces or government-supported militias or bands have engaged in "ethnic cleansing"—forced removal or killing of undesired ethnic groups. Hundreds of thousands of victims were killed, raped, or otherwise affected by wars in the former Yugoslavia in Europe and Congo in Africa, and in genocidal ethnic conflicts in Rwanda and Sudan in Africa. Many observers argued that human rights were being violated on such a massive scale that they threatened the stability and peace of neighboring regions.

> Some of the greatest human rights problems have been not the product of repressive governments but of failed states and social breakdown related to civil war and ethnic conflict.

In 2001 a special independent commission sponsored by the United Nations released a study arguing that the responsibility to protect all people from gross human rights abuses could justify foreign military intervention. The study states, "Sovereign states have a responsibility to protect their own citizens from avoidable catastrophe—from mass murder and rape, from starvation—but . . . when they are unwilling or unable to do so, that responsibility must be borne by the broader community of states."[35]

The UN General Assembly voted to approve the "Responsibility to Protect" or R2P principle in 2005. However, the UN Security Council, which has actual authority to order military intervention, has been slow to act on it. Perhaps the most noteworthy current test of the R2P principle is in Sudan, a northern African nation wracked by prolonged civil war, whose government has been complicit in significant human rights crimes (including possible genocide) against populations in the Darfur region. For several years the Security Council resisted even debating the situation in Sudan (China, a permanent member of the Council, has shouldered much if not all the blame for the council's inaction; the Chinese government has extensive oil and business dealings with the Sudanese government). Resolution 1769, finally passed by the Security Council in 2007, authorized a peacekeeping force (UNAMID) of 20,000 African Union soldiers and 6,000 UN police to enter the Darfur region and protect populations from atrocities. The resolution is seen by some as a pioneering development for UN action on human rights. However, implementation of UNAMID has been hampered by the Sudanese government's lack of cooperation, lagging financial support for equipment and helicopters, and questions about whether the force will be big enough to make a difference. Meanwhile, other ongoing conflicts in the Congo, Sri Lanka, Afghanistan, and other places raise their own challenges to the UN's self-proclaimed "Responsibility to Protect" populations from gross human rights abuses.

> " Some globalization critics argue that the free trade agreements countries sign may actually violate human rights treaties previously ratified. "

Justice and the International Criminal Court

The UN record is arguably better in after-the-fact accounting for human rights violations. In 1993 and 1994 it established 2 temporary international tribunals to try suspects in Yugoslavia and Rwanda. The tribunals had some success in bringing abusers and leaders to justice. In 1998 nations negotiated the Rome Statute, creating a permanent international criminal court (ICC) that began operations in 2002. Designed to prosecute human rights abusers and other significant international lawbreakers, the ICC has issued several indictments, including one against the president of Sudan, but has not begun any actual trials in the first 6 years of its existence.

Human Rights and Globalization

A very different challenge for human rights supporters is globalization and its effects. Globalization refers to the phenomenon of the world becoming more interconnected through increased trade of goods, services, and money; the growing migrations of people across national borders; and the linking of people across borders via telecommunications and the Internet. Globalization is also sometimes equated with the capitalist free trade policies promoted by the United States and by world bodies such as the World Bank and the World Trade Organization (WTO).

Globalization has several ramifications for human rights. Some argue that globalization, especially free trade, is itself a positive development for human rights. "Governments that grant their citizens a large measure of freedom to engage in international commerce find it increasingly difficult to deprive them of political liberties, while governments that 'protect' their citizens behind tariff walls and other barriers to international commerce find it much easier to deny those same liberties," argues Daniel T. Griswold, a trade policy scholar at the Cato Institute. "The correlation between economic openness and political freedom . . . is not perfect, but the broad trends are undeniable," Griswold notes.[36]

> " Concern about human rights violations committed by what are called 'nonstate actors' has been growing. "

However, others believe that globalization harms the cause of human rights. They argue that when developing countries embrace globalization by pursuing free trade and market-based economic policies, they may be hurting their citizens so much as to violate their human rights. Free trade policies, in this view, may protect profits of foreign investors

> **By raising consciousness about . . . human rights . . . the hope is that from seemingly hopeless situations a new generation of activists will use this knowledge as a powerful tool for reform.**

and transnational corporations and benefit local elites. At the same time, these policies may leave millions of people without important economic and social rights, including adequate food, safe water, affordable medicine, and/or work opportunities at fair wages. Some globalization critics argue that the free trade agreements countries sign may actually violate human rights treaties previously ratified. "Globalization policies have clearly gone against the spirit and the letter of international human rights treaties," argues the Asian Pacific Research Network, an organization of Asian NGOs. The organization recommends that both rich and poor nations rework their trade and economic policies in a way that is "accountable to their binding human rights obligations."[37]

Nonstate Actors

Globalization has also raised the question of the human rights responsibilities of private corporations and other nongovernmental entities. UN human rights treaties are signed by governments, which are seen as having primary responsibility for their implementation. However, concern about human rights violations committed by what are called "nonstate actors" has been growing. Activists have accused corporations such as Nike, Coca Cola, and Chevron Oil of such violations as employing underage children or exploiting forced labor; complicity and cooperation with governments and police forces in suppressing freedoms of speech, press, and association; irreparably harming the environment; and other actions contrary to human rights standards. The UN has come up with various codes of conduct for corporations, a development that, according to Amnesty International, is part of "a clear trend to extend human rights obligations beyond states, including to individuals (for international crimes), armed groups, international organizations, and private enterprises."[38]

Human Rights and Social Problems

Human rights concerns have been cited in more and more social and political movements. Many activists have embraced human rights both as a tool for educating people and as a legal and political instrument for forcing change in government policies. Silvano M. Tomasi, a Roman Catholic archbishop and UN observer, argues that human rights provide a moral foundation for possible solutions to many important issues: "Without a guarantee of the dignity of the individual person, issues of security, terrorism, freedom of religion and belief, poverty, the environment, and similar themes . . . cannot be properly and effectively dealt with."[39]

Shortly after becoming secretary-general of the UN in 1997, Kofi Annan directed the various agencies under his control to formally incorporate human rights concerns in their work, be it in economic development, disease control, population growth, refugees, the environment, or other specialties. A 2000 report by the UN Development Programme (UNDP) provides one example of how a UN agency has embraced human rights arguments. The primary function of the UNDP is to help the world's poorest nations in their social and economic development. In the report the UNDP stated that its goals of a

> decent standard of living, adequate nutrition, health care, and other social and economic achievements are not just development goals. They are human rights inherent in human freedom and dignity. But these rights do not mean an entitlement to a handout. They are claims to a set of social arrangements—norms, institutions, laws, an enabling economic environment—that can best secure the enjoyment of these rights. It is thus the obligation of governments and others to implement policies to put these arrangements in place.[40]

Similar reorientations placing goals in the context of human rights have been done in other UN organizations and in other private and public groups working on social issues.

Human Rights Education

A related development has been a greater focus on human rights education for the general population. For decades a standard image of a human rights activist has been a person from America or other Western nation writing a letter to a third-world dictator asking for the release of a political prisoner, or a group of outsiders investigating and criticizing foreign countries for human rights violations. However, more recently a growing number of organizations have sought to change this dynamic and build grassroots support for human rights at the local level. Many have worked closely with marginalized populations, such as the very poor, refugees, women, and children. These people, who suffer from pervasive social discrimination, often do not know or have little use for human rights laws and treaties. But by raising consciousness about the human rights they (like everyone) have, the hope is that from seemingly hopeless situations a new generation of activists will use this knowledge as a powerful tool for reform.

The true future of human rights activism may be on this local level, according to some. "Some people speak of 'international human rights' as though it were a single word, as though the rights cannot be talked about separately from the international framework," notes activist Scott Long. "But rights do not begin at the international level. They begin with local problems and local lives, with individuals who realize their dignity has been injured, and strive to imagine remedies and solutions."[41]

Thus, a growing number of individuals and organizations are working at the grassroots community level to promote and protect human rights. This is occurring even as other organizations continue to lobby and work with the United Nations Security Council to promote greater international cooperation in human rights enforcement. "To a degree almost unimaginable in 1948," asserts Amnesty International in its 2008 annual report, "today there is a global citizens' movement that is demanding their leaders recommit themselves to upholding and promoting human rights."[42] Whether at the local, national, or international levels, those inspired by the vision of the Universal Declaration of Human Rights continue to strive for its realization.

What Is the Future of Human Rights?

66 **For the past three decades, globalization, human rights, and democracy have been marching forward together.** 99

—Daniel T. Griswold, "Globalization, Human Rights, and Democracy," *eJournalUSA*, February 2006. http://usinfo.state.gov.

Griswold is director of the Center for Trade Policy Studies at the Cato Institute in Washington, D.C.

66 **The rights to food, work, health, and education . . . are among the most fundamental and inalienable human rights that have been systematically violated as a result of the World Trade Organization (WTO).** 99

—Asian Pacific Research Network, "APRN Statement on Human Rights and Trade: The WTO's Decade of Human Rights Violations," December 10, 2005. www.aprnet.org.

The Asian Pacific Research Network is a group of nongovernmental research organizations; the network strives to share and exchange information on international issues.

Bracketed quotes indicate conflicting positions.

* Editor's Note: While the definition of a primary source can be narrowly or broadly defined, for the purposes of Compact Research, a primary source consists of: 1) results of original research presented by an organization or researcher; 2) eyewitness accounts of events, personal experience, or work experience; 3) first-person editorials offering pundits' opinions; 4) government officials presenting political plans and/or policies; 5) representatives of organizations presenting testimony or policy.

66 **Human rights problems are not isolated tragedies, but are like viruses that can infect and spread rapidly, endangering all of us.** 99

—Irene Khan, quoted in Amnesty International, "Sixty Years of Human Rights Failure—Government Must Apologize and Act Now," press release, May 27, 2008. www.amnesty.org.

Khan is secretary-general of Amnesty International.

66 **International failure in responding to genocide in Darfur should be occasion for the deepest shame.** 99

—Eric Reeves, "Failure to Protect: International Response to Darfur Genocide." *Harvard International Review*, Winter 2008.

Reeves is a professor of English language and literature at Smith College in Massachusetts. He has spent the past nine years as a Sudan researcher and analyst and is the author of *A Long Day's Dying: Critical Moments in the Darfur Genocide*.

66 **Legal history shows that it takes centuries rather than decades for new legal concepts to take full effect. From this perspective, international human rights protection is still in its infancy.** 99

—Walter Kälin, *The Face of Human Rights*. Baden, Switzerland: Lars Müller, 2004.

Kälin is a law professor at the University of Bern in Switzerland and a frequent consultant to various United Nations agencies on human rights.

66 **Access to rights for the very poor and excluded represents a challenge to human rights organizations. Establishing and monitoring the law is not enough.** 99

—International Council on Human Rights Policy, *Enhancing Access to Human Rights*. Vernier, Switzerland: Atar Roto Press, 2004.

The International Council on Human Rights Policy is an organization established by the United Nations to provide studies and analyses on how human rights can be protected.

66 The sovereignty of States must no longer be used as a shield for gross violations of human rights. 99

—Kofi Annan, Nobel Peace Prize lecture, December 10, 2001.

Annan, a diplomat from Ghana, Africa, served as secretary-general of the United Nations from 1997 to 2007 and won the Nobel Peace Prize in 2001.

66 Failed states clearly show that the protection of human rights is dependent on the proper functioning of the state. Human rights need to be given legislative shape and implemented internally, which necessitates functioning state bodies. 99

—Daniel Thurer, "An Internal Challenge: Partnerships in Fixing Failed States," *Harvard International Review*, Winter 2008.

Thurer is a professor of international law and comparative law at the University of Zurich, Switzerland.

66 In areas of violent conflict and instability, the pursuit of profits without human rights safeguards can fuel a range of abuses, including torture, forced labor, war crimes, and crimes against humanity. 99

—Lisa Misol, "Private Companies and the Public Interest: Why Corporations Should Welcome Global Human Rights Rules," in Human Rights Watch, *World Report 2006*. New York: Seven Stories, 2006.

Misol is a researcher with the Business and Human Rights Program at Human Rights Watch.

66 What the human rights community faces now is not a problem of acceptance, but of continually nourishing the idea and seeing to it that they are made real in everyday life the world over. 99

—John Tirman, *100 Ways America Is Screwing Up the World*. New York: HarperCollins, 2006.

Tirman is executive director of the Massachusetts Institute of Technology's Center for International Studies.

66 In the coming decades, human rights campaigns will increasingly have to be directed against companies, not countries. The demand is simple: Basic liberties must not stop at the workplace door. **99**

—Jason Mark, "At the Millennium, a Broader Definition of Human Rights: Justice, Democracy, and Dignity," Global Exchange, January 2001. www.globalexchange.org.

Jason Mark is a human rights activist.

....

66 Multinationals such as Shell and McDonald's have been vilified in recent years. Surely, it is a source of consternation to them that they are sometimes blamed for problems that are really the responsibility of the host government. **99**

—Daniel Litvin, "Needed: A Global Business Code of Conduct," *Foreign Policy*, November/December 2003.

Litvin is director of a London-based firm that provides analyses to businesses on ethical issues and is the author of *Empires of Profit: Commerce, Conquest, and Social Responsibility.*

....

66 Like teaching slaves to read in 19th-century America, teaching human rights in 21st-century America is a far-reaching act that offers a rich vision of human possibilities. **99**

—Loretta Ross, quoted in Julie A. Mertus, "Bait and Switch? Human Rights and U.S. Foreign Policy," *FPIF Policy Report*, Foreign Policy in Focus, March 2004.

Ross is founder and director of the National Center for Human Rights Education, a Georgia-based nonprofit corporation that trains social and political activists in global human rights law.

....

66 I don't want my daughters to suffer the way I have, and so I need to learn how to protect my rights and theirs. **99**

—Anonymous, quoted in Amnesty International, "Broken Promises," *Amnesty International Report 2008*.

An anonymous woman villager in Bangladesh explains why she is taking a legal literacy class on marriage laws and other civil rights matters.

....

Facts and Illustrations

What Is the Future of Human Rights?

- Since 2002, an estimated **300,000–400,000** people in the Darfur region in Sudan have been killed and more than 2 million driven from their homes.

- In 2008 Sudanese president Omar al Bashir was indicted for **genocide** by the chief prosecutor of the International Criminal Court.

- More than **1 billion people** in the world live in severe poverty (income of less than one dollar a day).

- An estimated **8 million** people around the world die every year because of poverty—they are too poor to stay alive.

- Of the estimated **50,000** multinational corporations in the world, an estimated 50 have internal codes of conduct that refer explicitly to global human rights standards.

- South Asia has an estimated **10 million slaves** (workers held in debt bondage).

- The United States was one of seven nations to vote against the formation of an **International Criminal Court**. The other six nations were China, Iraq, Israel, Libya, Qatar, and Yemen.

- After five plus years of operation, the International Criminal Court had issued **12 indictments** for war crimes and crimes against humanity and had four people in custody, but had yet to begin a trial.

Facts and Illustrations

Number of Free Countries Growing

According to Freedom House, a private human rights group that assesses the state of political and civil rights around the world, the percentage of the world's population that live in free countries has grown substantially since 1976.

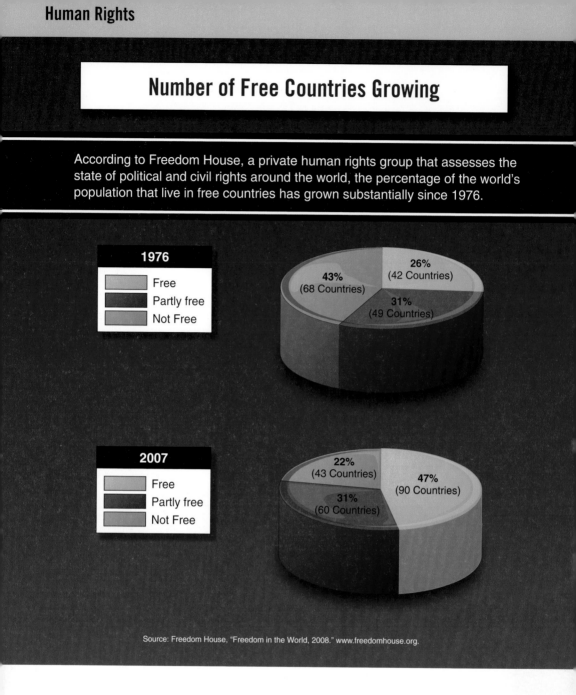

1976

- Free
- Partly free
- Not Free

26%
(42 Countries)

43%
(68 Countries)

31%
(49 Countries)

2007

- Free
- Partly free
- Not Free

22%
(43 Countries)

47%
(90 Countries)

31%
(60 Countries)

Source: Freedom House, "Freedom in the World, 2008." www.freedomhouse.org.

- The International Labor Organization estimates that **246 million** children between the ages of 5 and 17 currently work (or about **15 percent** of the world's children, about **35 percent** of children in Sub-Saharan Africa).

Slavery Remains a Serious Human Rights Problem Today

Although slavery and other forms of involuntary servitude are prohibited in multiple UN covenants and declarations, modern slavery remains a serious and hard-to-measure problem in many parts of the world. Below are examples of places where various forms of slavery persist.

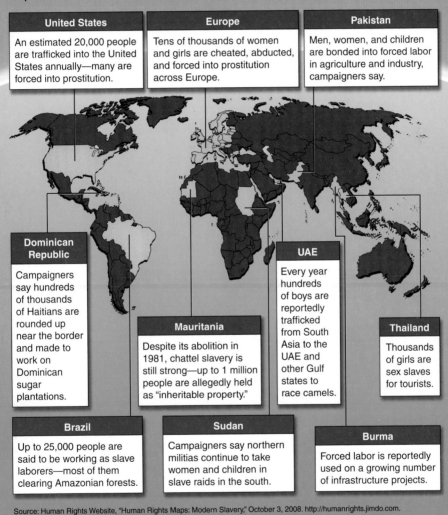

United States

An estimated 20,000 people are trafficked into the United States annually—many are forced into prostitution.

Europe

Tens of thousands of women and girls are cheated, abducted, and forced into prostitution across Europe.

Pakistan

Men, women, and children are bonded into forced labor in agriculture and industry, campaigners say.

Dominican Republic

Campaigners say hundreds of thousands of Haitians are rounded up near the border and made to work on Dominican sugar plantations.

Mauritania

Despite its abolition in 1981, chattel slavery is still strong—up to 1 million people are allegedly held as "inheritable property."

UAE

Every year hundreds of boys are reportedly trafficked from South Asia to the UAE and other Gulf states to race camels.

Thailand

Thousands of girls are sex slaves for tourists.

Brazil

Up to 25,000 people are said to be working as slave laborers—most of them clearing Amazonian forests.

Sudan

Campaigners say northern militias continue to take women and children in slave raids in the south.

Burma

Forced labor is reportedly used on a growing number of infrastructure projects.

Source: Human Rights Website, "Human Rights Maps: Modern Slavery," October 3, 2008. http://humanrights.jimdo.com.

- According to the International Labor Organization, more than **12 million** people worldwide are forced into labor. Approximately **77 percent** are found in Asia and the Pacific Islands.

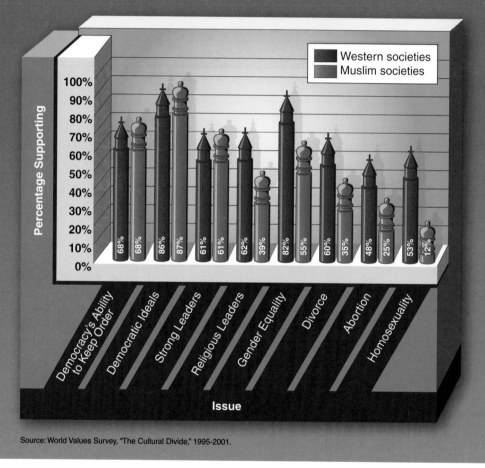

Western and Muslim Opinions on Human Rights Issues

A comprehensive poll taken by the World Values Survey found that while Muslims value democracy and strong leaders, they are less tolerant of gender equality, homosexuality, abortion, and divorce.

Western societies
Muslim societies

Percentage Supporting

100%
90%
80%
70%
60%
50%
40%
30%
20%
10%
0%

68% 68% 86% 87% 61% 61% 62% 39% 82% 55% 60% 35% 48% 25% 53% 12%

Democracy's Ability to Keep Order
Democratic Ideals
Strong Leaders
Religious Leaders
Gender Equality
Divorce
Abortion
Homosexuality

Issue

Source: World Values Survey, "The Cultural Divide," 1995-2001.

- In 2007, the UN Security Council authorized a peacekeeping force of **20,000** African Union solders and **6,000** UN police to enter Darfur and protect vulnerable populations from atrocities.

Key People and Advocacy Groups

Amnesty International: AI is a worldwide volunteer movement with more than 2 million members and donors in more than 150 countries. Founded in 1961, its original mission was the freeing of political prisoners and the abolition of torture and executions; it has expanded its focus to include violence against women, poverty, and other human rights problems.

Kofi Atta Annan: Annan, a diplomat from Ghana, Africa, served as secretary-general of the United Nations from 1997 to 2007. His tenure was marked by strong vocal support for human rights as a "pillar" of United Nations principles and by a reorganization of UN offices and bodies dealing with human rights.

Peter Benenson: Benenson, a British lawyer and human rights activist, founded Amnesty International in 1961.

Jimmy Carter: Carter, president of the United States from 1977 to 1981, placed a new emphasis on human rights in formulating U.S. foreign policy and has continued to promote human rights as a private citizen through the Carter Center.

René Samuel Cassin: A French jurist and scholar, Cassin was a member of the United Nations Commission on Human Rights from 1946 to 1959. He was a member of the committee that wrote the Universal Declaration of Human Rights and composed the first full draft of the declaration.

Shirin Ebadi: Born in Tehran, Iran in 1947, Ebadi became the first female judge in that country. Following the 1979 Islamic revolution, she went into private practice and became a leading advocate of human rights in the Muslim world. She won the Nobel Prize for Peace in 2003.

Freedom House: Freedom House is a private organization that promotes democratic values. It surveys and publishes annual reports rating all the world's nations on civil and political liberties.

Václav Havel: A writer and human rights activist, Havel was jailed and imprisoned after signing Charter 77, a document protesting Czechoslovakia's refusal to abide by human rights commitments. He later became president of Czechoslovakia and (later) the Czech Republic, and continued to work for the human rights of ethnic minorities in the Czech Republic and central Europe.

Human Rights Watch: Founded in 1978 to help local groups in the Soviet Union and Eastern Europe monitor government compliance with human rights agreements, the nongovernmental organization has expanded and now conducts regular and thorough investigations of human rights abuses in 70 countries worldwide. Its publications include the influential annual *World Report*.

International Labour Organization: The ILO was founded in 1919; in 1945 it became a specialized agency within the United Nations. The Geneva-based organization promotes basic labor rights such as freedom of association, the right to organize unions, and freedom from servitude and forced labor.

Juan E. Mendez: An Argentine lawyer and teacher, Mendez was imprisoned without charges by the country's military government in 1976 and exiled in 1977. He later worked for Americas Watch (now Human Rights Watch/Americas), investigating and reporting on human rights abuses in Latin America. He also has worked for the Inter-American Commission on Human Rights and as a special adviser on the prevention of genocide for the United Nations.

Aryeh Neier: Neier, president of the Open Society Institute, is a long-time activist for human rights, especially civil and political rights. He served 12 years as executive director of Human Rights Watch and eight years as head of the American Civil Liberties Union.

Office of the United Nations High Commissioner for Human Rights: The office, established in 1993, is the main human rights agency of the UN Secretariat, the executive branch of the United Nations. It works for the universal ratification and implementation of all UN human rights treaties.

Mary Robinson: One of the world's most prominent voices on behalf of human rights, Robinson served as president of Ireland from 1990 to 1997 and United Nations high commissioner for human rights from 1997 to 2002. She later founded the Ethical Globalization Initiative.

Eleanor Roosevelt: Wife of President Franklin D. Roosevelt and long-time humanitarian, Roosevelt was appointed a delegate to the United Nations in 1945 by President Harry Truman. She chaired the UN Commission on Human Rights from 1946 to 1951, where she played a major part in the drafting of the Universal Declaration of Human Rights.

Chronology

1945
The United Nations is established.

1961
Amnesty International is founded.

1946
UN Commission on Human Rights is established; begins work on human rights declaration.

1966
UN General Assembly votes to adopt the International Covenant on Civil and Political Rights (ICCPR) and the International Covenant on Economic, Social and Cultural Rights (ICSCR).

1949
The Geneva Conventions are adopted by the UN to ensure decent treatment for prisoners of war and prohibit their torture or mistreatment.

1945   1955   1965   1975

1953
Secretary of State John Foster Dulles announces that the United States will not let itself be legally bound by any United Nations human rights agreements.

1959
European Court of Human Rights is established to enforce human rights conventions for the Council of Europe. The Organization of American States creates the Inter-American Commission on Human Rights to monitor human rights situations in member states.

1967
UN Commission on Human Rights initiates procedures for receiving and investigating human rights complaints.

1948
The UN adopts the Convention on the Prevention and Punishment of the Crime of Genocide. The Universal Declaration of Human Rights is adopted by the General Assembly.

1975
Human rights provisions are included in Helsinki Accord signed by 35 Western and Eastern European countries, the Soviet Union, United States, and Canada.

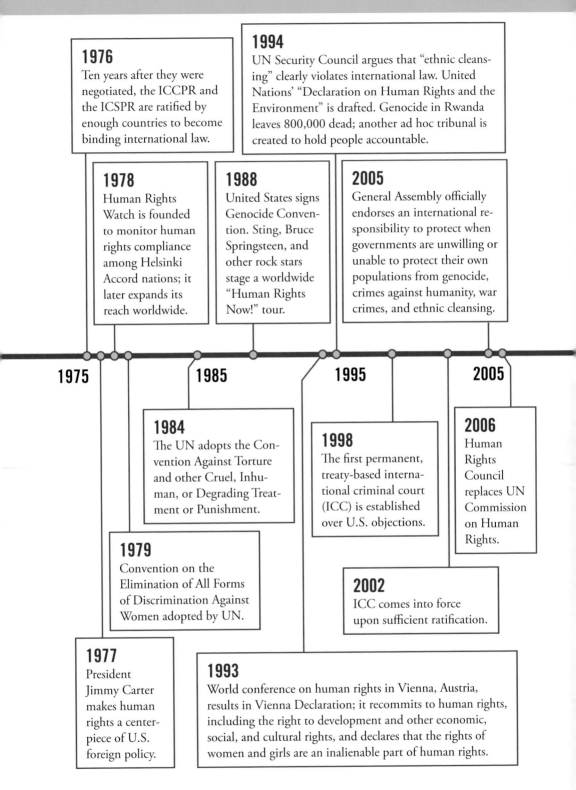

1976
Ten years after they were negotiated, the ICCPR and the ICSPR are ratified by enough countries to become binding international law.

1994
UN Security Council argues that "ethnic cleansing" clearly violates international law. United Nations' "Declaration on Human Rights and the Environment" is drafted. Genocide in Rwanda leaves 800,000 dead; another ad hoc tribunal is created to hold people accountable.

1978
Human Rights Watch is founded to monitor human rights compliance among Helsinki Accord nations; it later expands its reach worldwide.

1988
United States signs Genocide Convention. Sting, Bruce Springsteen, and other rock stars stage a worldwide "Human Rights Now!" tour.

2005
General Assembly officially endorses an international responsibility to protect when governments are unwilling or unable to protect their own populations from genocide, crimes against humanity, war crimes, and ethnic cleansing.

1975

1985

1995

2005

1984
The UN adopts the Convention Against Torture and other Cruel, Inhuman, or Degrading Treatment or Punishment.

1998
The first permanent, treaty-based international criminal court (ICC) is established over U.S. objections.

2006
Human Rights Council replaces UN Commission on Human Rights.

1979
Convention on the Elimination of All Forms of Discrimination Against Women adopted by UN.

2002
ICC comes into force upon sufficient ratification.

1977
President Jimmy Carter makes human rights a centerpiece of U.S. foreign policy.

1993
World conference on human rights in Vienna, Austria, results in Vienna Declaration; it recommits to human rights, including the right to development and other economic, social, and cultural rights, and declares that the rights of women and girls are an inalienable part of human rights.

Related Organizations

Advocates for Human Rights

650 Third Ave. South, Suite 550

Minneapolis, MN 55402

phone: (612) 341-3302 • fax: (612) 341-2971

Web site: www.theadvocatesforhumanrights.org

Advocates for Human Rights is a nongovernmental organization that works to promote human rights and prevent human rights violations. It documents human rights abuses, advocates on behalf of human rights victims, and provides education and training materials on human rights for school and community classes.

American Enterprise Institute (AEI)

1150 Seventeenth St. NW

Washington, DC 20026

phone: (202) 862-5800 • fax: (202) 862-7117

Web site: www.aei.org

AEI is a public policy institute that works to preserve limited government, private enterprise, and a strong U.S. foreign policy. It has published several articles supportive of U.S. intervention for human rights and critical of the United Nations.

Amnesty International USA (AIUSA)

5 Penn Plaza, 14th Floor

New York, NY 10001

phone: (212) 807-8400 • fax: (212) 627-1451

e-mail: aimember@aiusa.org • Web site: www.amnestyusa.org

AIUSA is the United States section of Amnesty International, a worldwide organization that campaigns for internationally recognized human rights. It publishes *Amnesty Magazine* and the annual *State of the World* human rights reports.

The Carter Center

One Copenhill, 453 Freedom Pkwy.

Atlanta, GA 30307

phone: (800) 550-3560

e-mail: carterweb@emory.edu • Web site: www.cartercenter.org

Founded in 1982 by former U.S. president Jimmy Carter and former First Lady Rosalynn Carter, the Carter Center sponsors programs and activities to advance the cause of human rights. Its Web site provides news about its activities, including its support of local human rights activists; it also provides background information on human rights, democracy, and conflict resolution.

Center for Economic and Social Rights (CESR)

162 Montague St., 3rd Floor

Brooklyn, NY 11201

phone: (718) 237-9145 • fax: (718) 237-9147

e-mail: rights@cesr.org • Web site: http://cesr.org

CESR was established in 1993 to promote social justice through human rights strategies and advocates economic and social rights as expressed in the Universal Declaration of Human Rights. It uses multidisciplinary tools to measure how nations are upholding their treaty commitments to provide housing, health, education, food, and other rights. CESR publishes various articles and reports.

Dai Hua Foundation

450 Sutter St., Suite 900

San Francisco, CA 94108

Established in 1999, the Dai Hua Foundation works to advance human rights protection in China and the United States by supporting a dialogue based on mutual respect between the two nations.

Equality Now

PO Box 20646, Columbus Circle Station

New York, NY 10023

fax: (212) 586-1611

e-mail: info@equalitynow.org • Web site: www.equalitynow.org

Equality Now is an international human rights organization dedicated to action for the civil, political, economic, and social rights of girls and women and to promote women's rights at local, national, and international levels. The organization publishes the quarterly update *Words and Deeds*.

Ethical Globalization Initiative (EGI)

271 Madison Ave., Suite 1007

New York, NY 10016

phone: (212) 895-8080 • fax: (212) 895-8084

e-mail: info@eginitiative.org • Web site: www.realizingrights.org

The Ethical Globalization Initiative, founded in 2002, seeks to ensure that the needs of the poorest and most vulnerable peoples and nations are met and that human rights standards shape global trade, development, and migration policies.

Evangelicals for Human Rights (EHR)

3001 Mercer University Dr., Day Hall 103

Atlanta, GA 30341-4115

phone: (678) 547-6457 • fax: (678) 547-6409

e-mail: ehr@nrcat.org • Web site: www.evangelicalsforhumanrights.org

EHR is a group that works to raise awareness among evangelical Christians of torture and degrading treatment of terrorist detainees and to deepen their commitment to human rights. It produced "An Evangelical Declaration Against Torture: Protecting Human Rights in an Age of Terror," a joint statement drafted by 17 evangelical leaders and signed by thousands of Christians.

Human Rights First (NRF)

333 Seventh Ave., 13th Floor

New York, NY 10001-5108

phone: (212) 845 5200 • fax: (212) 845 5299

Web site: www.humanrightsfirst.org

Founded in 1978 as the Lawyer's Committee on Human Rights, HRF provides legal and other assistance to people at risk, including refugees, war crimes victims, victims of discrimination, and others whose human rights have been violated. It publishes and provides informational resources on its Web site.

Human Rights Watch

350 Fifth Ave., 34th Floor

New York, NY 10118-3299

phone: (212) 290-4700 • fax: (212) 736-1300

e-mail: hrwnyc@hrw.org • Web site: www.hrw.org

Human Rights Watch is an independent, nongovernmental organization dedicated to protecting human rights. It investigates human rights violations and works to hold abusers accountable. It publishes annual reports on human rights conditions around the world.

International Council on Human Rights Policy (ICHRP)

Chemin du Grand-Montfleury 48, PO Box 147

1290 Versoix

Switzerland

phone: +41 (0) 22 775 33 00 • fax: +41 (0) 22 775 33 03

e-mail: info@ichrp.org • Web site: www.ichrp.org

The ICHRP was established in 1998 in Geneva, Switzerland, to conduct applied research into current human rights issues. Its studies are designed to provide practical advice to governments, regional and international organizations, and volunteer groups working to secure human rights. Reports include *Access to Rights* and *Negotiating Justice? Human Rights and Peace Treaties*.

People's Decade for Human Rights Education (PDHRE)

526 W. 111th St., Suite 4E

New York, NY 10025

phone: (212) 749-3156 • fax: (212) 666-6325

e-mail: pdhre@igc.org • Web site: www.pdhre.org

Founded in 1988, PDHRE is a nonprofit international service organization that works with women's and social justice organizations to develop and advance teaching materials and methods to make human rights relevant to people's daily lives. It has offices and affiliate organizations around the world.

Physicians for Human Rights

2 Arrow St., Suite 301

Cambridge, MA 02138

phone: (617) 301-4200 • fax: (617) 301-4250

Web site: www.physiciansforhumanrights.org

Physicians for Human Rights is an organization of health professionals and specialists that works to promote the right to health for all. Members also investigate human rights abuses. Its publications include the report *Broken Laws, Broken Lives: Medical Evidence of Torture by US Personnel and Its Impact*.

Washington Office on Latin America (WOLA)

1666 Connecticut Ave. NW, Suite 400

Washington, DC 20009

phone: (202) 797-2171 • fax: (202) 797-2172

Web site: www.wola.org

WOLA promotes human rights, democracy, and social and economic justice in Latin America and the Caribbean. It facilitates dialogue between governmental and nongovernmental actors, monitors the impact of policies and programs of governments and international organizations, and promotes alternatives through reporting, education, training, and advocacy. Founded in 1974 by a coalition of civic and religious leaders, WOLA works closely with civil society organizations and government officials throughout the Americas.

World Programme for Human Rights Education

OHCHR, Palais des Nations

CH-1211 Geneva 10, Switzerland

phone: +41 (0) 22 9289304 • fax: +41 (0) 22 9289061

e-mail: wphre@ohchr.org

The programme was established by the UN General Assembly in 2004 to create and disseminate strategies and ideas for implementing human rights education programs and to promote basic principles and methodologies of human rights education.

Youth for Human Rights International (YHRI)

1954 Hillhurst Ave., # 416

Los Angeles, CA 90027

phone: (323) 663-5799

e-mail: info@youthforhumanrights.org

Web site: www.youthforhumanrights.org

YHRI is an independent private organization that seeks to educate people about the Universal Declaration of Human Rights and to train people to be advocates of tolerance and peace. It produces instructional tools and materials on human rights, including the *UNITED Human Rights Handbook*.

For Further Research

Books

Zehra F. Kabasakal Arat, *Human Rights Worldwide: A Reference Handbook*. Santa Barbara, CA: ABC-CLIO, 2006.

Olivia Ball, *The No-Nonsense Guide to Human Rights*. Oxford: New Internationalist, 2006.

Maria S. Becker and Julia N. Schneider, eds., *Human Rights Issues in the 21st Century*. New York: Nova Science, 2008.

John Bowe, *Nobodies: Modern American Slave Labor and the Dark Side of the New Global Economy*. New York: Random House, 2007.

Alice Bullard, ed., *Human Rights in Crisis*. Burlington, VT: Ashgate, 2008.

Rhonda L. Callaway and Julie Harrelson-Stephens, eds., *Exploring International Human Rights: Essential Readings*. Boulder, CO: Lynne Rienner, 2007.

Helen Fein, *Human Rights and Human Wrongs: Slavery, Terror, Genocide*. Boulder, CO: Paradigm, 2007.

Daniel Fischlin and Martha Nandorfy, *The Concise Guide to Global Human Rights*. New York: Black Rose, 2007.

James Griffin, *On Human Rights*. New York: Oxford University Press, 2008.

Jan Hancock, *Human Rights and U.S. Foreign Policy*. New York: Routledge, 2007.

John M. Headley, *The Europeanization of the World: On the Origins of Human Rights and Democracy*. Princeton, NJ: Princeton University Press, 2008.

Walter Kälin et al., eds., *The Face of Human Rights*. Baden, Switzerland: Lars Müller, 2004.

Pradyumma Karan, *The Non-Western World: Environment, Development and Human Rights*. New York: Routledge, 2004.

Murat Kurnaz, *Five Years of My Life: An Innocent Man in Guantánamo*. New York: Palgrave Macmillan, 2008.

Paul A. Marshall, ed., *Religious Freedom in the World*. Lanham, MD: Rowman & Littlefield, 2008.

Julie A. Mertus, *Bait and Switch: Human Rights and U.S. Foreign Policy*. New York: Routledge, 2008.

Mahmood Monshipouri et al., *Constructing Human Rights in the Age of Globalization*. New York: M.E. Sharpe, 2003.

Paul J. Nelson and Ellen Dorsey, *New Rights Advocacy: Changing Strategies of Development and Human Rights NGOs*. Washington, DC: Georgetown University Press, 2008.

Thomas Pogge, ed., *Freedom from Poverty as a Human Right: Who Owes What to the Very Poor?* New York: Oxford University Press, 2007.

Anthony George Ravlich, *Freedom from Our Social Prisons: The Rise of Economic, Social, and Cultural Rights*. Lanham, MD: Lexington, 2008.

Mary Robinson, *A Voice for Human Rights*. Philadelphia: University of Pennsylvania Press, 2006.

Philippe Sands, *Torture Team: Rumsfeld's Memo and the Betrayal of American Values*. New York: Palgrave Macmillan, 2008.

William F. Schulz, *Tainted Legacy: 9/11 and the Ruin of Human Rights*. New York: Thunder's Mouth/Nation, 2003.

Steve Tsang, ed., *Intelligence and Human Rights in the Era of Global Terrorism*. Westport, CT: Praeger Security International, 2007.

Periodicals

Commonweal, "What About Darfur?" January 26, 2007.

Theodore Dalrymple, "Second Opinion," *Spectator*, February 4, 2006.

Economist, "A Screaming Start; The UN and Human Rights," April 26, 2008.

Michael D. Goldhaber, "The Death of Alien Tort: Can Corporations Be Liable for Aiding and Abetting Human Rights Abuses Abroad? An Appellate Battle over Apartheid Reparations Could Be High Noon for the Alien Tort," *American Lawyer*, July 2006.

Kermit D. Johnson, "Inhuman Behavior: A Chaplain's View of Torture," *Christian Century*, April 18, 2006.

Charles Krauthammer, "The Truth About Torture: It's Time to Be Honest About Doing Terrible Things," *Weekly Standard*, December 5, 2005.

Anthony Lewis, "Official American Sadism," *New York Review of Books*, September 25, 2008.

Joseph Loconte, "A Bad Day for Human Rights," *Weekly Standard*, December 11, 2007.

Shadi Mokhtari, "Human Rights in the Post–September 11 Era: Between Hegemony and Emancipation," *Muslim World Journal of Human Rights*, 2006.

New Internationalist, "Human Rights—the Facts," January/February 2008.

Leslie Palti, "Combating Terrorism While Protecting Human Rights," *UN Chronicle*, vol. 41, no. 4, 2004.

Eyal Press, "Rights of Passage," *Nation*, December 31, 2007.

Eric Reeves, "Failure to Protect: International Response to Darfur Genocide," *Harvard International Review*, Winter 2008.

Kenneth Roth, "Ending Lapse into Lawlessness," *World Today*, August 2008.

E. Benjamin Skinner, "A World Enslaved," *Foreign Policy*, March/April 2008.

Desmond Tutu, "Peace and Human Rights," *Harvard International Review*, Spring 2008.

Washington Monthly, "No Torture. No Exceptions." January/February 2008.

Web Sites

Derechos Human Rights, www.derechos.org.

Human Rights Tribune, www.humanrights-geneva.info.

Know Your Rights. http://html.knowyourrights2008.org.

United Nations Human Rights Treaties, www.bayefsky.com.

University of Minnesota Human Rights Library, www1.umn.edu/humanrts.

Appendix

The Universal Declaration of Human Rights

Preamble

Whereas recognition of the inherent dignity and of the equal and inalienable rights of all members of the human family is the foundation of freedom, justice and peace in the world,

Whereas disregard and contempt for human rights have resulted in barbarous acts which have outraged the conscience of mankind, and the advent of a world in which human beings shall enjoy freedom of speech and belief and freedom from fear and want has been proclaimed as the highest aspiration of the common people,

Whereas it is essential, if man is not to be compelled to have recourse, as a last resort, to rebellion against tyranny and oppression, that human rights should be protected by the rule of law,

Whereas it is essential to promote the development of friendly relations between nations,

Whereas the peoples of the United Nations have in the Charter reaffirmed their faith in fundamental human rights, in the dignity and worth of the human person and in the equal rights of men and women and have determined to promote social progress and better standards of life in larger freedom,

Whereas Member States have pledged themselves to achieve, in co-operation with the United Nations, the promotion of universal respect for and observance of human rights and fundamental freedoms,

Whereas a common understanding of these rights and freedoms is of the greatest importance for the full realization of this pledge,

Now, therefore, The General Assembly proclaims this Universal Declaration of Human Rights as a common standard of achievement for all peoples and all nations, to the end that every individual and every organ of society, keeping this Declaration constantly in mind, shall strive by teaching and education to promote respect for these rights and freedoms and by progressive measures, national and international, to secure their universal and effective recognition and observance, both among the peoples of Member States themselves and among the peoples of territories under their jurisdiction.

Article 1

All human beings are born free and equal in dignity and rights. They are endowed with reason and conscience and should act towards one another in a spirit of brotherhood.

Article 2

Everyone is entitled to all the rights and freedoms set forth in this Declaration, without distinction of any kind, such as race, color, sex, language, religion, political or other opinion, national or social origin, property, birth or other status.

Furthermore, no distinction shall be made on the basis of the political, jurisdictional or international status of the country or territory to which a person belongs, whether it be independent, trust, non-self-governing or under any other limitation of sovereignty.

Article 3

Everyone has the right to life, liberty and the security of person.

Article 4

No one shall be held in slavery or servitude; slavery and the slave trade shall be prohibited in all their forms.

Article 5

No one shall be subjected to torture or to cruel, inhuman or degrading treatment or punishment.

Article 6

Everyone has the right to recognition everywhere as a person before the law.

Article 7

All are equal before the law and are entitled without any discrimination to equal protection of the law. All are entitled to equal protection against any discrimination in violation of this Declaration and against any incitement to such discrimination.

Article 8

Everyone has the right to an effective remedy by the competent national tribunals for acts violating the fundamental rights granted him by the constitution or by law.

Article 9

No one shall be subjected to arbitrary arrest, detention or exile.

Article 10

Everyone is entitled in full equality to a fair and public hearing by an independent and impartial tribunal, in the determination of his rights and obligations and of any criminal charge against him.

Article 11

1. Everyone charged with a penal offence has the right to be presumed innocent until proved guilty according to law in a public trial at which he has had all the guarantees necessary for his defense.

2. No one shall be held guilty of any penal offence on account of any act or omission which did not constitute a penal offence, under national or international law, at the time when it was committed. Nor shall a heavier penalty be imposed than the one that was applicable at the time the penal offence was committed.

Article 12

No one shall be subjected to arbitrary interference with his privacy, family, home or correspondence, nor to attacks upon his honor and reputation. Everyone has the right to the protection of the law against such interference or attacks.

Article 13

1. Everyone has the right to freedom of movement and residence within the borders of each state.

2. Everyone has the right to leave any country, including his own, and to return to his country.

Article 14

1. Everyone has the right to seek and to enjoy in other countries asylum from persecution.

2. This right may not be invoked in the case of prosecutions genuinely arising from non-political crimes or from acts contrary to the purposes and principles of the United Nations.

Article 15

1. Everyone has the right to a nationality.

2. No one shall be arbitrarily deprived of his nationality nor be denied the right to change his nationality.

Article 16

1. Men and women of full age, without any limitation due to race, nationality or religion, have the right to marry and to found a family. They are entitled to equal rights as to marriage, during marriage and at its dissolution.

2. Marriage shall be entered into only with the free and full consent of the intending spouses.

3. The family is the natural and fundamental group unit of society and is entitled to protection by society and the State.

Article 17

1. Everyone has the right to own property alone as well as in association with others.

2. No one shall be arbitrarily deprived of his property.

Article 18

Everyone has the right to freedom of thought, conscience and religion; this right includes freedom to change his religion or belief, and freedom, either alone or in community with others and in public or private, to manifest his religion or belief in teaching, practice, worship and observance.

Article 19

Everyone has the right to freedom of opinion and expression; this right includes freedom to hold opinions without interference and to seek, receive and impart information and ideas through any media and regardless of frontiers.

Article 20

1. Everyone has the right to freedom of peaceful assembly and association.

2. No one may be compelled to belong to an association.

Article 21

1. Everyone has the right to take part in the Government of his country, directly or through freely chosen representatives.

2. Everyone has the right of equal access to public service in his country.

3. The will of the people shall be the basis of the authority of government; this will shall be expressed in periodic and genuine elections which shall be by universal and equal suffrage and shall be held by secret vote or by equivalent free voting procedures.

Article 22

1. Everyone, as a member of society, has the right to social security and is entitled to realization, through

national effort and international cooperation and in accordance with the organization and resources of each State, of the economic, social and cultural rights indispensable for his dignity and the free development of his personality.

Article 23

1. Everyone has the right to work, to free choice of employment, to just and favorable conditions of work and to protection against unemployment.

2. Everyone, without any discrimination, has the right to equal pay for equal work.

3. Everyone who works has the right to just and favorable remuneration insuring for himself and his family an existence worthy of human dignity, and supplemented, if necessary, by other means of social protection.

4. Everyone has the right to form and to join trade unions for the protection of his interests.

Article 24

Everyone has the right to rest and leisure, including reasonable limitation of working hours and periodic holidays with pay.

Article 25

1. Everyone has the right to a standard of living adequate for the health and well-being of himself and of his family, including food, clothing, housing and medical care and necessary social services, and the right to security in the event of unemployment, sickness, disability, widowhood, old age or other lack of livelihood in circumstances beyond his control.

2. Motherhood and childhood are entitled to special care and assistance. All children, whether born in or out of wedlock, shall enjoy the same social protection.

Article 26

1. Everyone has the right to education. Education shall be free, at least in the elementary and fundamental stages. Elementary education shall be compulsory. Technical and professional education shall be made generally available and higher education shall be equally accessible to all on the basis of merit.

2. Education shall be directed to the full development of the human personality and to the strengthening of respect for human rights and fundamental freedoms. It shall promote understanding, tolerance and friendship among all nations, racial or religious groups, and shall further the activities of the United Nations for the maintenance of peace.

3. Parents have a prior right to choose the kind of education that shall be given to their children.

Article 27

1. Everyone has the right freely to participate in the cultural life of the community, to enjoy the arts and to share in scientific advancement and its benefits.

2. Everyone has the right to the protection of the moral and material interests resulting from any scientific, literary or artistic production of which he is the author.

Article 28

Everyone is entitled to a social and international order in which the rights and freedoms set forth in this Declaration can be fully realized.

Article 29

1. Everyone has duties to the community in which alone the free and full development of his personality is possible.

2. In the exercise of his rights and freedoms, everyone shall be subject only to such limitations as are determined by law solely for the purpose of securing due recognition and respect for the rights and freedoms of others and of meeting the just requirements of morality, public order and the general welfare in a democratic society.

3. These rights and freedoms may in no case be exercised contrary to the purposes and principles of the United Nations.

Article 30

Nothing in this Declaration may be interpreted as implying for any State, group or person any right to engage in any activity or to perform any act aimed at the destruction of any of the rights and freedoms set forth herein.

Hundred and eighty-third plenary meeting
Resolution 217(A)(III) of the United Nations General Assembly,
December 10, 1948

Source Notes

Overview

1. Winston E. Langley, *Encyclopedia of Human Rights Issues Since 1945*. Westport, CT: Greenwood, 1999, p. 144.
2. Langley, *Encyclopedia of Human Rights Issues Since 1945*, p. 145.
3. Quoted in Alan Dershowitz, *Rights from Wrongs: A Secular Theory of the Origins of Rights*. New York: Basic Books, 2004, pp. 1–2.
4. Quoted in Dershowitz, *Rights from Wrongs*, p. 24.
5. Quoted in Dershowitz, *Rights from Wrongs*, p. 2.
6. Dershowitz, *Rights from Wrongs*, p. 23.
7. William Shulz, *Tainted Legacy*. New York: Thunder's Mouth/Nation, 2003, pp. 110–11.
8. Universal Declaration of Human Rights, GA res. 217A (III), UN Doc A/810 at 71 (1948).
9. Quoted in *The New Encyclopedia Britannica*, 15th ed., s.v. "Human Rights."

What Are Human Rights?

10. Gerald S. Snyder, *Human Rights*. New York: Franklin Watts, 1980, p. 3.
11. Quoted in Snyder, *Human Rights*, p. 3.
12. Julie Harrelson-Stephens and Rhonda L. Callaway, "What Are Human Rights?" in Julie Harrelson-Stephens and Rhonda L. Callaway, eds. *Exploring International Human Rights: Essential Readings*. Boulder, CO: Lynne Rienner, 2007, p. 4.
13. Harrelson-Stephens and Callaway, pp. 4–5.
14. Human Rights Watch, *World Report 2008*, p. 350.
15. Human Rights Watch, *World Report 2008*, p. 350.
16. Amnesty International, *Amnesty International Report 2008*, p. 4.
17. Quoted in Xiaorong Li, "'Asian Values' and the Universality of Human Rights," *Report from the Institute for Philosophy and Public Policy*, Spring 1996.
18. René V. Sarmiento, "Human Rights: Universal? Indivisible? Interdependent?" speech delivered in Quezon City, Philippines, June 20, 1995. www.hrsolidarity.net.

How Can Global Human Rights Best Be Protected?

19. Gil Loescher with Ann Loescher, *Human Rights*. New York: E.P. Dutton, Loescher, 1978, p. 104.
20. Amnesty International, "Broken Promises," foreword, *Amnesty International Report 2008*, p. 13.
21. Newt Gingrich, *Winning the Future*. Washington, DC: Regnery, 2005, p. 15.
22. Joseph Loconte, "The United Nations' Disarray: The Decline of the Human-Rights Agenda, and What Evangelicals Can Do About It," *Christianity Today*, vol. 51, February 2007.
23. James Traub, *The Best Intentions: Kofi Annan and the UN in the Era of American World Power*. New York: Farrar, Straus, and Giroux, 2006.

Should U.S. Foreign Policy Consider Human Rights?

24. Jimmy Carter, inaugural address, January 20, 1977, in John T. Woolley and Gerhard Peters, The American Presidency Project. University

of California, Santa Barbara. www.presidency.ucsb.edu.

25. Quoted in Snyder, *Human Rights*, p. 7.

26. Quoted in Roberta Cohen, "Integrating Human Rights in US Foreign Policy," address before Foreign Service Institute, 2008.

27. Bureau of Democracy, Human Rights, and Labor, "Saudi Arabia," *Country Reports on Human Rights Practices—2007*, U.S. State Department, March 11, 2008.

28. Bureau of Near Eastern Affairs, "Background Note: Saudi Arabia," U.S. State Department, February 2008. www.state.gov.

29. Bureau of Near Eastern Affairs, "Background Note: Saudi Arabia."

30. Julie A. Mertus, *Bait and Switch: Human Rights and U.S. Foreign Policy*. New York: Routledge, 2008, p. 84.

31. Quoted in Sangitha McKenzie Millar, "Extraordinary Rendition, Extraordinary Mistake," *Foreign Policy in Focus*, August 29, 2008.

32. Jack Goldsmith, *The Terror Presidency*. New York: Norton, 2007, p. 59.

33. Mark Bowden, "The Dark Art of Interrogation," *Atlantic Monthly*, October 2003.

What Is the Future of Human Rights?

34. Roger Normand and Sarah Zaidi, *Human Rights at the UN: The Political History of Universal Justice*. Bloomington: Indiana University Press, 2007, p. 340.

35. International Commission on Intervention and State Sovereignty, *Responsibility to Protect*. Ottawa, ON: International Development Research Centre, December 2001, p. 14.

36. Daniel T. Griswold, "Globalization, Human Rights, and Democracy," *eJournalUSA*, February 2006. http://usinfo.state.gov.

37. Asian Pacific Research Network, "APRN Statement on Human Rights and Trade: The WTO's Decade of Human Rights Violations," December 10, 2005. www.aprnet.org.

38. Amnesty International, *The UN Human Rights Norms for Business: Towards Legal Accountability*. London: Amnesty International, 2004, p. 7.

39. Silvano M. Tomasi, "United Nations Reform and Human Rights," *America*, vol. 193, September 12, 2005.

40. United Nations Development Programme, *Human Development Report 2000: Human Rights and Human Development*, p. 73.

41. Quoted in Julie A. Mertus, *The United Nations and Human Rights*. New York: Routledge, 2005, p. 4.

42. Amnesty International, "Broken Promises."

List of Illustrations

List of Illustrations

Index

Africa, prevalence of female genital mutilation in, 48 (map)
African Charter on Human and People's Rights (1981), 40
American Convention on Human Rights (1969), 40
American Revolution (1776), 13, 22
Amnesty International, 8, 16, 24, 30, 35, 44
  on actions of countries infringing on human rights, 31
  on future of human rights, 66
  on global human rights movement, 72
  size of, 46
Amon, Joseph, 28
Annan, Kofi, 39, 71, 75
Arbor, Louise, 29
Asian Pacific Research Network, 70, 73
Association for World Education, 30
Association of World Citizens, 30

al Bashir, Omar, 77
Bentham, Jeremy, 14
Bowden, Mark, 56
Bowles, Newton R., 43
Bureau of Democracy, Human Rights, and Labor (DRL), 51, 61
Bush, George W., 12, 45, 51, 52
  on torture, 59
  waives sanctions on Saudi Arabia for human rights violations, 54
  war on terror and, 54–55

Cairo Declaration of Human Rights, 30
Callaway, Rhonda L., 21
Carter, Jimmy, 16–17, 50–51
child labor, prevalence of, 78
children, street, numbers globally, 63
China, abuses of human rights of Tibetan by, 25–26
Commission on Human Rights, UN, 38–39
Convention Against Torture, UN, 55
Convention on Children's Rights, UN, 61
conventions (covenants), UN, vs. declarations, 38
criminal trials, number of countries conducting unfair, 31

Dafur (Sudan)
  authorization of UN peacekeeping force

in, 68
  deaths in/refugees from, 77
death penalty, nations leading in use of, 47 (chart)
Declaration of Independence (1776), 9, 13
Declaration on the Rights of Indigenous Peoples, UN, 36
declarations, UN, conventions (covenants) vs., 38
Dershowitz, Alan, 8, 12
Dobriansky, Paula, 50

Economist (magazine), 20
education, on human rights, 18–19, 71–72
ethnic cleansing, 67
European Convention for the Protection of Human Rights and Fundamental Freedoms, 40

failed states, 6–7
Falk, Richard A., 43
female genital mutilation, in Africa, prevalence of, 48 (map)
free speech, number of countries restricting, 31
French Revolution (1789), 13, 22

General Assembly, UN, 36
  approves Responsibility to Protect (R2P) principle, 68
Gingrich, Newt, 39
global economy, human rights and, 7
globalization, 18
  human rights and, 69–70
Goldsmith, Jack, 56
Griswold, Daniel T., 69, 73
Guantánamo Bay prison (Cuba), 55, 56
  numbers detained in/released from, 64

Hamilton, Alexander, 12
Haroon, Abdullah Hussain, 30
Harrelson-Stephens, Julie, 21
Holocaust, 9–10
human rights
  debates over categories of, 26–27
  definitions of, 20–21
  first-generation, 22
    abuse of, 23–24
  future of, 17–18

About the Author

William Dudley received his degree in English from Beloit College, Wisconsin. He is a San Diego–based writer and editor. His work includes *Human Rights* and *Antidepressants* in the Compact Research series.